FAIRY TALE KNITS

20 ENCHANTING CHARACTERS TO MAKE

Andrews McMeel
Publishing, LLC

Kansas City · Sydney · London

Fairy Tale Knits

Copyright © Ivy Press Limited 2012

Andrews McMeel Publishing, LLC
an Andrews McMeel Universal company
1130 Walnut Street, Kansas City, Missouri 64106
www.andrewsmcmeel.com

ISBN: 978-1-4494–1801-4

Library of Congress Control Number:
2011944684

This book was conceived, designed, and produced by

Ivy Press
210 High Street
Lewes
East Sussex BN7 2NS
United Kingdom
www.ivypress.co.uk

Creative Director Peter Bridgewater
Publisher Sophie Collins
Editorial Director Tom Kitch
Senior Designer James Lawrence
Designer Andrew Milne
Photographer Andrew Perris
Illustrator Melvyn Evans

Printed in China

Color origination by Ivy Press Reprographics

12 13 14 15 16 IYP 10 9 8 7 6 5 4 3 2 1

**ATTENTION:
SCHOOLS AND BUSINESSES**

Andrews McMeel books are available at quantity discounts with bulk purchase for educational, business, or sales promotional use. For information, please e-mail the Andrews McMeel Publishing Special Sales Department: specialsales@amuniversal.com

IMPORTANT!
Safety warning: The knitted figures are not toys. Many have small, removable parts and should be kept out of the reach of small children.

Contents

Introduction

Some stories are here today and gone tomorrow, but fairy tales have been adored and remembered by generation after generation of children—and by grown-ups, too.

In addition to brand-new versions of six favorite fairy tales, this book contains directions so you can create your own troupe of twenty knitted characters to bring the tales to life with some drama and glamor.

Of course, the book features fairy-tale stars such as the precocious Goldilocks and the coquettish Rapunzel. However, there are also knitting patterns to help you make beloved members of the supporting cast, including those notorious sisters from "Beauty and the Beast," evil Dame Gothel, Little Red Riding Hood's sweet granny, and the fearsome cross-dressing wolf.

Why do fairy tales continue to be so popular? It's not just that we all love a handsome hero, such as Rapunzel's prince, and a happy ending.

The stories in this book are packed with hardship, cruelty, and danger lurking in familiar places, as the fairy-tale innocents Hansel, Gretel, and Little Red Riding Hood discover. However, as the stories show, with some quick thinking and a little good fortune, enemies such as the horrible hag in "Hansel and Gretel," the devious wolf in "Little Red Riding Hood," and the wicked witch who imprisoned poor, beautiful Rapunzel *can* be overcome.

Just in case you think modern living has become a little superficial and sloppy, one of the tales in this book will help everyone understand that you really shouldn't take what isn't yours, as the three woolly bears demonstrated to Goldilocks. And be forewarned: If you don't act sensibly, a fate similar to that of two of the three little pink pigs may be yours. Finally, as Beauty eventually realizes when the beast removes his mask, if you judge a book entirely by its cover, you could be missing a real gem.

Check Out Your Knitting Bag

Even if you've only knitted a few projects before, you probably have most of what you need for these projects already in your knitting bag. However, to avoid the frustration of getting everything ready to begin only to realize there's something missing, here is a list of all essential items.

☑ Knitting Needles

You will need ordinary knitting needles (sometimes called single-pointed needles) in three sizes to make all the projects in this book.

Because the dolls are small and you will not have many stitches on your needles at any one time, you will find shorter needles easier to work with. It's also a good idea to choose needles with somewhat pointed ends. The projects in this book are more tightly knitted than most garments, and using pointed needles will make it easier to get the right gauge.

A PAIR OF SIZE U.S. 2 (2.75 MM)
You will need these to knit a few of the accessories, for example, the dolls' shoes.

A PAIR OF SIZE U.S. 2/3 (3 MM)
These are the basic needles that you will use to create the dolls and most of their outfits. If you think that you knit more tightly or more loosely than normal, you may need slightly larger or smaller needles, so look at the guide to gauge on page 7 to make sure.

A PAIR OF SIZE U.S. 5 (3.75 MM)
You will need these to knit some of the characters' clothes.

☑ A Crochet Hook

You will need a size D-3 (3.25 mm) or similar size crochet hook to make crochet chains for some of the dolls' clothes and hair.

☑ A Needle to Sew Together Your Work

You will need a needle with a fairly blunt end and an eye large enough for threading yarn to sew together your dolls. Sometimes, these are called "yarn needles," but a tapestry needle will do the job just as well.

☑ An Embroidery Needle

You will need an embroidery needle with an eye large enough for threading yarn to embroider your dolls' features. Embroidery needles are sharper than tapestry or yarn needles, and having a sharp needle will make it much easier to work the necessary stitches.

☑ An Ordinary Sewing Needle

You will need this to sew the buttons, beads, and sequins onto your dolls' clothes.

☑ A Stitch Holder, Large Safety Pin, or Spare Knitting Needle

For some of the projects, you'll need somewhere to hold spare stitches while you work on a different section of your knitting. You can choose a special knitting stitch holder or use a spare needle or large safety pin.

☑ A Measuring Tape or Ruler

You'll need a measuring tape or ruler to measure lengths of yarn or the length of crochet chains.

☑ A Pair of Small Scissors

These are essential for trimming the yarn tails after you have sewn together your work.

☑ Glue

You will probably find it easier to glue one or two of the trimmings in place, instead of sewing them on. Any PVA glue that dries clear is suitable for this.

☑ Red and Pink Colored Pencils

The cheeks of the dolls are colored by rubbing over the finished knitting with an ordinary colored pencil. Don't be tempted to use a crayon or a felt-tipped pen, because the results will be disappointing.

☑ A Water-Soluble Pen

This looks and works like an ordinary felt-tipped pen, but the ink disappears when it is sprayed or dabbed with water. Water-soluble pens are very useful for marking the position of dolls' features before embroidering them. Before you use your pen, test it on the type of yarn you have used in the project to make sure that the ink comes out easily.

☑ A Row Counter

You can get several different types of row counters to help you keep track of how many rows you have worked. Some people find this useful, but it isn't essential.

☑ Yarns

All the dolls and their clothes in this book are knitted in double knitting (DK) yarn. Yarn is available in 100 percent wool, 100 percent acrylic, or a mix of wool and acrylic. It can also be made from fibers such as cotton, silk, or bamboo—or from these fibers mixed with wool and acrylic. It is recommended that you use either 100 percent wool yarns or wool mixes (wool mixed with acrylic or other fibers). Cotton yarns and 100 percent acrylic yarns can lead to disappointing results.

For some of the projects in this book, you'll also need small amounts of mohair yarn, bulky yarn, and metallic crochet yarn.

☑ Buttons, Beads, Bows, and Sequins

Some of the dolls are adorned with a few small items such as buttons and beads. The ones recommended are only suggestions; feel free to raid your sewing box to find inspiration for embellishing your creations.

☑ Snap Fasteners

For a few of the projects, you'll need some small snap fasteners. You can use either plastic or metal snaps.

☑ Polyester Toy Filling

The dolls are stuffed with a 100 percent polyester filling that is specially made for stuffing handmade items such as toys. Be sure that the filling you buy conforms to safety standards.

☑ Sewing Thread

You'll need some standard sewing thread to sew on buttons, beads, and sequins.

ABBREVIATIONS

The following abbreviations are used in the knitting patterns in this book.

*/**	these mark the start and end of a section of the knitting pattern to be repeated later when instructed	sl	slip one (slip a stitch onto the right-hand needle without knitting it)
( )	repeat the directions within the parentheses the number of times indicated	psso	pass slipped stitch over (pass the slipped stitch over the stitch just knitted)
[ ]	number in brackets refers to how many stitches you should have on your needle	ssk	slip, slip, knit (slip 2 stitches kwise, one at a time, then knit the 2 slipped stitches together through the back loop)
K	knit		
P	purl	rs	right side
st(s)	stitch(es)	ws	wrong side
st st	stockinette stitch	alt	alternate
beg	beginning	yo	yarn over (bring the yarn from the back of the work to the front, then over the top of the needle)
cont	continue		
k2tog	knit the next 2 stitches together		
p2tog	purl the next 2 stitches together	rem	remaining
		rep	repeat
kwise	knitting or as to knit	g	gram
pwise	purling or as to purl	oz.	ounce
incl	increase one stitch (by knitting into the front and back of the same stitch)	mm	millimeter
		cm	centimeter
		in.	inch
ml	make one stitch (by picking up the horizontal loop before the next stitch and knitting into the back of it)	m	meter
		yd.	yard

GAUGE

The general knitting gauge for the patterns in this book is 12 sts and 16 rows to 1½ in. (4 cm) square in st st on U.S. 2/3 (3 mm) needles.

With the dolls, gauge is not as crucial as when knitting a garment. However, if your knitting is too loose, your dolls may end up looking shapeless and the stuffing may show through.

Knitting Fundamentals

Y ou don't need to know any complicated knitting techniques to knit the projects in this book. If you know how to knit and purl, to cast on and bind off, and to increase and decrease, you'll find the instructions straightforward. If you need to brush up on any of these techniques, read on.

Casting On

You can cast on in several different ways but the recommended way, which gives your knitting a firm edge, is called a cable cast on and uses two needles.

1 Make a slip knot by forming a loop in the yarn. With your knitting needle, pull a second loop of yarn through this loop. Then pull the knot up tightly. This slip knot forms the first cast-on stitch.

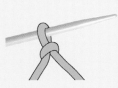

2 Hold the needle with the slip knot in your left hand. Hold the other needle in your right hand and insert the point through the slip knot and under the left needle. Wind the yarn attached to the ball (not the yarn tail) around the tip of the right needle.

3 Using the point of the right needle, draw the yarn through the slip knot to form a loop.

4 Transfer the loop, which is your new stitch, onto the left needle. You will now have two stitches on the left needle.

5 To make the next stitch, insert the right needle between the two stitches on the left needle and wind the yarn over the right needle from left to right.

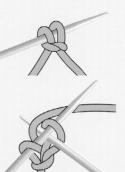
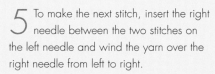

6 With the right needle, draw the yarn through the gap between the stitches to form a loop. Transfer the loop onto the left needle. There will now be three cast-on stitches on your needle.

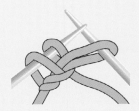

Repeat the last two steps until you have the required number of stitches on your needle.

The Knit Stitch

This is the basic knitting stitch.

1 To make your first knit stitch, hold the needle with the cast-on stitches in your left hand and check that the working end of the yarn is at the back of the work. Insert the point of the right needle into the front of the first cast-on stitch, from left to right.

2 Wind the yarn around the point of the right needle, from left to right.

3 Using the tip of the right needle, pull the yarn through the original stitch to form a loop on the right needle.

4 Slip the original stitch off the left needle by gently pulling the right needle to the right. The new stitch is now on this needle.

Repeat the four steps above until you have knitted all the stitches on the left needle. To knit the next row, turn the work, transferring the needle from your right to your left hand.

The Purl Stitch

Purling a stitch is like working a knit stitch backward. Working alternate rows of knit and purl stitches creates a stitch known as stockinette stitch, which is the main stitch used in this book. Purl stitches are generally worked with the reverse side of your work facing you, while knit stitches are worked on the right side of the work.

1 To make your first purl stitch, hold the needle with the stitches in your left hand and check that the working end of the yarn is at the front of the work. Insert the right needle through the front of the first stitch on the left needle from right to left.

2 Wind the yarn around the needle from right to left.

3 With the tip of the right needle, pull the yarn through the original stitch to form a loop on the needle.

4 Slip the original stitch off the left needle by gently pulling the right needle farther to the right. The new stitch will now be on this needle.

Repeat the four steps above until you have purled all the stitches on the left needle. To work the next row, turn the work, transferring the needle from your right to your left hand.

Binding Off

When you have finished your knitting, you will need to bind off to prevent the knitting from unraveling. Try not to bind off too tightly, because this can make it harder to sew together the knitted pieces.

BINDING OFF KNITWISE

The steps below describe how to bind off knitwise. This is the normal method for binding off on the right side of your work and also sometimes on the reverse side. If the pattern does not tell you to bind off in a specific way, you should bind off knitwise.

1 Knit two stitches in the normal way. Using the tip of the left needle, pick up the first stitch that you knitted and lift it over the second stitch.

2 You now have just one stitch on the right needle; you can see that there is a neat loop across the top of the first bound-off stitch, so the yarn cannot unravel.

Knit another stitch, so that you have two stitches on the right needle once more, and lift the first stitch over the second. Repeat this process until you have only one stitch left on the right needle. Trim the yarn, leaving a tail long enough to sew together your knitting. Pull the yarn tail all the way through the last stitch.

BINDING OFF PURLWISE

Sometimes you will need to bind off purlwise. Binding off purlwise is like binding off knitwise, except that you purl the stitches instead of knitting them.

1 Purl two stitches in the normal way. Using the point of the left needle, pick up the first stitch that you purled and lift it over the second stitch.

2 As with binding off knitwise, you now have just one stitch on the right needle.

Purl another stitch, so that you have two stitches on the right needle once more, and lift the first stitch over the second. Repeat this process until you have only one stitch left on the right needle. Trim the yarn, leaving a tail long enough to sew together your knitting. Pull the yarn tail all the way through the last stitch.

Increasing

Knitted pieces are shaped by increasing or decreasing the number of stitches on your needle as you knit. There are different ways of doing this, and the method that you need will vary from project to project. The aim is to always make the increase as neat as possible.

INCREASING BY MAKING AN ADDITIONAL STITCH (M1)

1 At the point where you want the new stitch, pick up the horizontal strand that runs between the two stitches, using the tip of your right needle.

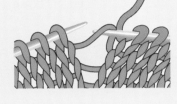

2 Transfer the strand to the left needle by inserting the tip of the left needle from right to left through the front of the strand.

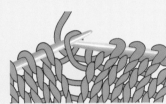

3 Knit through the back of the new stitch and transfer the stitch to your right needle.

INCREASING BY KNITTING INTO THE FRONT AND BACK OF THE SAME STITCH (INC1)

Start by knitting the stitch in the normal way. However, instead of slipping the old stitch off the needle, knit it again through the back before sliding it off. The instruction "inc1" refers to both creating the additional stitch and knitting the original stitch.

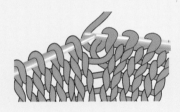

Decreasing

DECREASING BY KNITTING TWO STITCHES TOGETHER (K2TOG)

To knit two stitches together, simply insert your needle through the front of two stitches instead of one, and then knit them in the normal way.

DECREASING BY PURLING TWO STITCHES TOGETHER (P2TOG)

To purl two stitches together, simply insert your needle through the front of two stitches instead of one, and then purl them in the normal way.

DECREASING BY SLIPPING 2 STITCHES, THEN KNITTING THEM TOGETHER (SSK)

Slip one stitch and then the next stitch kwise onto the right needle, without knitting them. Insert the left needle from left to right through the front loops of both slipped stitches and knit them through the back loops.

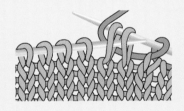

DECREASING TWO STITCHES AT A TIME (S1, K2TOG, PSSO)

1 Slip the first stitch from the left to the right needle kwise without knitting it. Knit together the next two stitches.

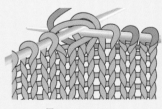

2 Using the point of the left needle, lift the slipped stitch over the stitch in front.

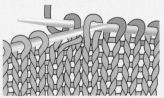

Sometimes you'll need to work this decrease on the wrong side of your work. In this case, simply slip the stitch purlwise, then purl together the next two stitches before passing the slipped stitch over.

Fancy Stitches

The main stitches that you'll need for this book are garter stitch (knit every row), stockinette stitch (alternate rows of knit and purl stitches), and ribbing (knit one stitch and purl the next). You'll also need to know eyelet stitch and extended garter stitch.

Eyelet Stitch

This stitch creates a knitted row with a series of holes. It can be used to produce a lacy effect or can be folded across the holes to create a wavy or picot edge. The holes can also be used for threading through a tie or cord.

On the right side of your work, bring the yarn to the front, under the right needle, then over the top (yarn over).

Knit together the next two stitches.

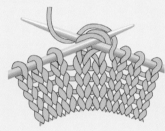

Extended Garter Stitch

For some items, you'll need to work a special version of garter stitch.

1 Insert the right needle into the stitch as if knitting the stitch normally. Instead of winding the yarn once around the needle, wind it around two or three times, as indicated in the pattern.

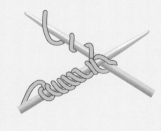

2 Continue knitting the stitch in the normal way, pulling all the loops through the stitch.

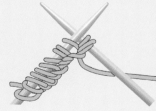

The row after the "extended" row is knitted in the normal way, dropping the extra loops as you go to create the extended sitch.

Crocheting a Chain

The projects don't involve much crochet, but you'll need to know how to make a simple crochet chain for some of the dolls and clothes.

1 Make a slip knot on the crochet hook, as if you were starting to cast on for knitting. Holding the slip stitch on the hook, wind the yarn around the hook from the back to the front, then catch the yarn in the crochet hook tip.

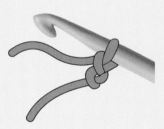

2 Pull the yarn through the slip stitch on the crochet hook to make the second link in the chain.

Continue in this way until the chain is the length that you need.

Reshaping

Sometimes the small garments that you create for your characters won't look exactly right. There is nothing wrong with your knitting—it's just that the items are small and yarns behave in certain ways. If you're not happy with the shape of a garment, simply soak the item in lukewarm water and squeeze it gently. Shape it while it is wet and let it dry.

Getting It Together

Piecing together your work is one of the best things about knitting the dolls in this book, because it's at this moment that you can really see your characters taking shape. Always join your knitted pieces using the same yarn that you used to knit your item, changing colors along the seam, if necessary. Take your time, particularly at first, to make sure that your work is neat and even.

Mattress Stitch

You can use one version of this stitch to join vertical seams and a different version to join horizontal edges. This joining technique produces a seam that is almost invisible.

VERTICAL EDGES

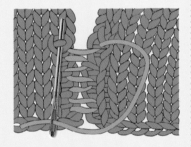

To join two vertical edges with mattress stitch, place the two pieces of knitting side by side. Take the needle under the running stitch between the first two stitches on one side, and then under the corresponding running stitch between the first two stitches on the other side. Continue in this way, pulling the yarn up fairly tightly every few stitches.

HORIZONTAL EDGES

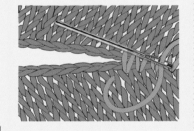

To join two horizontal edges, take the needle under the two "legs" of the last row of stitches on one piece of knitting, then under the two "legs" of the corresponding stitch on the other piece of knitting. Continue in this way, pulling the yarn up fairly tightly every few stitches.

You can use a variation of mattress stitch to join small pieces, such as limbs, to the main body.

Whipstitch

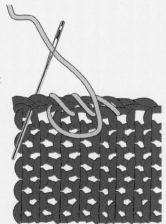

This is the best way to join together two small pieces at a seam or to join pieces with curved edges. It is normally worked with the right sides of the two pieces together.

The stitch is made by taking the needle from the front of your work, over the edge of the seam, and out through the front again.

A version of whipstitch is also used to join very small pieces of knitting, such as ears and shoes, to the main part of the doll.

Picking Up Stitches Along an Edge

Occasionally you'll need to pick up stitches along an edge and knit onto these stitches.

With the right side of the work facing you, insert the needle into the stitch where you need to begin picking up and knit into it the normal way.

Finishing Touches

Finishing your work in a neat and tidy way and adding just the right final touches can make all the difference to the look of your knitted items. So don't rush—be extra careful to get just the look that you want.

Hiding and Weaving in Ends

When you've finished knitting your items and sewing them together, there will probably be some yarn tails that need to be hidden.

For tails on the dolls, simply insert your needle into the body and bring it out at another point. Pull the yarn tightly and squash the body slightly, then trim the yarn close to the surface. When the body springs back into shape, the yarn tail will disappear into the middle of the doll and be invisible.

After knitting the dolls' clothes, weave in the ends by working a few small running stitches forward and then backward in the garment's seam, and then trim the yarn very close to the surface. You might want to use an embroidery needle for this and work into the threads, because this will help the yarn stay in place.

Embroidery

There are a few basic embroidery stitches you'll need to know in order to create your characters' features.

STARTING AND FINISHING

To start your embroidery, tie a simple knot at the end of the yarn. Insert the needle into the back of the work, between stitches in an inconspicuous area, then bring it out to the front at your starting point. Pull gently but firmly on the yarn, so that the knot slips through the stitches and embeds itself somewhere in the middle of the doll.

When you have finished your embroidery, bring the yarn out to an inconspicuous area and make a couple of very small stitches, one on top of the other, in the running stitches between the knitted stitches (these will be slightly sunken). Conceal the yarn end using the method described above.

STRAIGHT STITCH

This stitch is used for some of the characters' mouths and eyelashes. It is one of the easiest stitches and simply involves bringing the thread out at one point and down again at another point.

CHAIN STITCH

This embroidery stitch is used for the whites of the eyes, some of the noses, and some of the hair.

Bring the needle out at the point where you want the stitch to start. Then insert the needle back into the knitting, just next to the starting point, to create a little loop of yarn. Bring the needle back up through the knitting one stitch away and catch the loop. Pull the thread up gently until the stitch is firm.

FRENCH KNOT

This stitch is used for the pupils of the eyes and for the nostrils.

Bring the yarn out at the point where you want to work the knot. With the needle close to the surface of the knitting, wind the yarn twice around the needle. Insert the tip of the needle back into the knitting, just to the side of the starting point. Continue pulling the needle through the work and slide the knot off the needle and onto your knitting.

SATIN STITCH

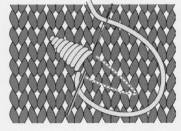

This stitch is used for some of the characters' noses and is really a series of straight stitches made very closely together.

Bring the needle out at the point where you want to start. Insert the needle back into the work and bring it out again near the starting point, ready to make the next stitch. Continue in this way until the shape is filled. To neaten the satin stitch, you can work a single straight stitch down the sides to conceal the beginning and end of each stitch.

Little Red Riding Hood

One day, Red Riding Hood's mother said to her, **"Now, Grandma has not been well—take this basket of treats to her and be back as fast as you can!"** Red Riding Hood went off through the forest. She wasn't certain of the trail, so she was relieved to meet a handsome stranger in a sleek fur coat. **"Please sir, I'm not too sure where my Grandma's house is . . ."** "Oh yes," said the Wolf, **"Go this way, little girl—it won't take long!"** As soon as she'd turned the corner, Wolfie sped around to Grandma's using a shortcut. He'd hatched a plan to eat the old lady and the little girl—and finish off with the basket of fruit and cakes. Yum yum! Leaping through the door, he gobbled up the old lady in a couple of gulps, slipped into her clothes (they were a little tight), and scrambled into bed, pulling the covers up high.

Not long after, Red Riding Hood came strolling through the door. "Hi, Grandma, are you feeling better?" "Yes," croaked the Wolf. "Why, Gran, what big ears you have!" (The Wolf's ears were, indeed, poking oddly out of Grandma's cap.) "All the better to hear you with!" cried the Wolf. "And your eyes . . . they're like saucers, and they're white . . ." "All the better to see you with!" shrilled the Wolf. "And your teeth . . . !" The Wolf couldn't contain himself any longer. "All the better to EAT you with!" he shouted, leaping from the bed.

Luckily, a nearby woodsman heard Red Riding Hood's loud screams and was at the door in a flash. He swung his ax and killed the Wolf with a couple of blows—releasing Grandma, who wasn't harmed by her experience. She warmed some milk on the stove and all three enjoyed a mug of hot chocolate before Red Riding Hood set off back home through the woods. "Good-bye darling!" called Grandma, waving from the door, "and remember—this time, don't talk to strangers!"

Little Red Riding Hood

She's wrapped up tightly in her brand new, wool coat, knitted in a stunning scarlet yarn. Now Little Red Riding Hood is ready to go over the river and through the woods with the basket of food for her ailing grandmother.

MATERIALS

$\frac{1}{16}$ oz./2 g (4½ yd./4 m) pale pink DK yarn

$\frac{1}{8}$ oz./3.5 g (9 yd./8 m) green DK yarn

¼ oz./6 g (15½ yd./14 m) flesh DK yarn

$\frac{1}{32}$ oz./1 g (3 yd./2.5 m) ocher DK yarn

$\frac{1}{8}$ oz./3.5 g (9½ yd./8.5 m) white DK yarn

¼ oz./7.5 g (20 yd./18 m) pale blue DK yarn

½ oz./15 g (37 yd./34 m) bright red DK yarn

$\frac{1}{16}$ oz./2 g (5½ yd./5 m) black DK yarn

Very small amount of mauve DK yarn

2 small white buttons

2 small snap fasteners

Red sewing thread

⅜–½ oz./10–15 g polyester toy filling

Red colored pencil

Use size U.S. 2/3 (3 mm) knitting needles except when instructed to use size U.S. 2 (2.75 mm) knitting needles.

DOLL

BODY AND HEAD

The body and head are knitted together from the bottom of the body up and include the underpants and top.

Front

Make 1

* Cast on 13 sts in pale pink.
* Work 7 rows in st st, beg with a K row.
* Next row: K.
* Break pale pink yarn and join green yarn.
* Work 11 rows in st st, beg with a K row.
* Next row: K.
* Break green yarn and join flesh yarn.
* Next row: K.
* Next row: (p2tog) twice, P to last 4 sts, (p2tog) twice. [9 sts]
* Next row: K1, inc1 into next 6 sts, K2. [15 sts]
* Next row: P.
* Next row: K1, inc1, K to last 3 sts, inc1, K2. [17 sts]
* Next row: P. *
* Rep last 2 rows twice more. [21 sts]
* Work 2 rows in st st, beg with a K row.
* Next row: K2, (k2tog) twice, K9, (ssk) twice, K2. [17 sts]
* Next row: p2tog, P to last 2 sts, p2tog. [15 sts]
* Next row: K2, (k2tog) twice, K3, (ssk) twice, K2. [11 sts]
* Next row: p2tog, P to last 2 sts, p2tog. [9 sts]
* Bind off.

Back

Make 1

* Work as for front to *.
* Break flesh yarn and join ocher yarn.
* Next row: K1, inc1, K to last 3 sts, inc1, K1. [19 sts]
* Next row: P.
* Rep last 2 rows once more. [21 sts]
* Work 2 rows in st st, beg with a K row.
* Next row: K2, (k2tog) twice, K9, (ssk) twice, K2. [17 sts]
* Next row: p2tog, P to last 2 sts, p2tog. [15 sts]

* Next row: K2, (k2tog) twice, K3, (ssk) twice, K2. [11 sts]
* Next row: p2tog, P to last 2 sts, p2tog. [9 sts]
* Bind off.

LEGS

The socks and legs are knitted as one piece, starting at the sole of the foot.
Make 2

* Cast on 20 sts in white.
* Work 4 rows in st st, beg with a K row.
* Next row: K5, bind off 10 sts, K5. [10 sts]
* Work 4 rows in st st, beg with a P row.
* Next row: K.
* Break white yarn and join flesh yarn.
* Work 10 rows in st st, beg with a K row.
* Bind off.

ARMS

The arms are knitted from the top of the shoulder to the tip of the hand.
Make 2

* Cast on 7 sts in green.
* Work 7 rows in st st, beg with a K row.
* Next row: K.
* Next row: P.
* Break green yarn and join flesh yarn.
* Work 11 rows in st st, beg with a P row.
* Next row: K1, k2tog, K1, ssk, K1. [5 sts]
* Next row: p2tog, P1, p2tog. [3 sts]
* Next row: s1, k2tog, psso. [1 st]
* Break yarn and pull it through rem st.

MAKING UP

With the front and back body and head pieces right sides together, whipstitch around the head. Turn the piece right side out and sew the side seams of the body using mattress stitch, leaving the lower edge open for stuffing. Stuff the doll and close the gap using mattress stitch.

Fold one leg in half lengthwise, right sides together, and whipstitch the top and lower edge of the foot. Turn the leg right side out and sew the long seam using mattress stitch. Repeat with the second leg. Stuff the legs and feet.

Fold one arm in half lengthwise, right sides together, and whipstitch around the hand. Turn the arm right side out and sew the long seam using mattress stitch. Repeat with the second arm. The arms do not need stuffing.

Sew the arms and legs in place.

Using ocher yarn, work a few rows of chain stitch at the front of the head for the hair. For the braids, cut a 16-in. (40-cm) length of ocher yarn. Hold the two yarn ends in one hand and insert your finger of the other hand in the loop. Holding the yarn taught, wind your finger to produce the cord. It will twist back on itself to produce a 4-strand cord. The twisted cords should be about 1.5 in. (4 cm) long. Work the second braid in the same way. Use the ends of the cord to fasten the braids to the sides of the head.

Work two French knots in black yarn for the eyes. Work two circles of chain stitch around each eye using white yarn. Using a single ply of black yarn, work three straight stitches above each eye for the eyelashes.

Work a small V-shaped mouth in straight stitches using mauve yarn. Add color to the cheeks using a red colored pencil.

SKIRT

Make 1

* Cast on 38 sts in pale blue.
* Work 3 rows in st st, beg with a P row.
* Leave pale blue yarn at side and join white yarn.
* K 2 rows. Break white yarn and use pale blue yarn.
* Work 8 rows in st st, beg with a K row.
* Next row: (k2tog) 9 times, K2, (ssk) 9 times. [20 sts]
* K 2 rows.
* Bind off.

MAKING UP

Sew the back seam of the skirt using mattress stitch.

COAT

The main part of the coat is knitted as one piece. The sleeves and hood are sewn on separately.

Make 1

❋ Cast on 28 sts in bright red.
❋ K 2 rows.
❋ Next row: K2, P6. Turn work and cont on only these 8 sts, leaving rem sts on needle.
❋ Next row: K.
❋ Next row: K2, P6.
❋ Rep these 2 rows once more.
❋ Break yarn and join it to rem sts on ws of work.
❋ Next row: P12. Turn work and cont on only these 12 sts, leaving rem sts on needle.
❋ Work 4 rows in st st, beg with a K row.
❋ Break yarn and join it to rem 8 sts on ws of work.
❋ Next row: P6, K2.
❋ Next row: K.
❋ Rep last 2 rows once more.
❋ Next row: P6, K2.
❋ Now work across all 28 sts.
❋ Next row: K6, m1, K4, m1, K8, m1, K4, m1, K6. [32 sts]
❋ Next row: K2, P to last 2 sts, K2.
❋ Next row: K.

❋ Next row: K2, P to last 2 sts, K2.
❋ Next row: K7, m1, K4, m1, K10, m1, K4, m1, K7. [36 sts]
❋ Next row: K.
❋ Next row: (K2, m1) to last 2 sts, K2. [53 sts]
❋ Next row: K2, P to last 2 sts, K2.
❋ Next row: K.
❋ Rep these 2 rows 6 times more.
❋ K 2 rows.
❋ Bind off.

SLEEVES

Make 2

❋ Cast on 12 sts in bright red.
❋ Work 13 rows in st st, beg with a K row.
❋ K 2 rows.
❋ Bind off.

HOOD

The hood is knitted from the face edge to the back.

Make 1

❋ Cast on 26 sts in bright red.
❋ K 2 rows.
❋ Work 15 rows in st st, beg with a P row.
❋ Bind off.

MAKING UP

Sew the seams of the sleeves using mattress stitch. Insert them into the armholes of the coat and whipstitch them in place from the inside.

Fold the hood piece in half widthwise and sew the back seam. Whipstitch the hood in place around the neck edge of the coat. The edges of the hood should come just to the front of the armhole edges.

Sew the buttons onto the right side of the coat. Sew the tops of the snap fasteners under the buttons and the bottoms of the snap fasteners to the corresponding part of the other side of the coat.

SHOES

Make 2

❋ Using size U.S. 2 (2.75 mm) needles, cast on 8 sts in black.
❋ 1st row: inc1, K to last 2 sts, inc1, K1. [10 sts]
❋ Next row: P.
❋ Rep last 2 rows once more. [12 sts]
❋ Next row: inc1, K to last 2 sts, inc1, K1. [14 sts]
❋ Next row: P5, bind off 4 sts pwise, P to end. Turn work and cont on only these last 5 sts, leaving rem sts on needle or on a safety pin.
❋ Work 6 rows in st st, beg with a K row.
❋ Bind off.
❋ With rs facing, rejoin yarn to rem sts.
❋ Work 6 rows in st st, beg with a K row.
❋ Bind off.

MAKING UP

Fold the shoe pieces in half lengthwise with the right side facing inward. Whipstitch the back and lower seam of the shoes. Turn the right way out. Put the shoes on the doll and secure with a couple of stitches. Work a couple of large straight stitches across the foot for the bar of the shoe.

HOW TO KNIT
The Grandmother

She may be getting on in years and not feeling too great at the moment, but most of the time Grandma enjoys life in her little home in the woods. Grandma often plays second fiddle to her famous granddaughter, but now you can help her shine by knitting your very own sweet little old lady in shades of yarn suited to her age.

DOLL

HEAD
The head is knitted from the base of the chin to the top of the forehead.
Make 2 pieces
❋ Cast on 6 sts in flesh.
❋ 1st row: K1, inc1, K2, inc1, K1. [8 sts]
❋ Next row: P.
❋ Next row: K1, m1, K to last st, m1, K1. [10 sts]
❋ Next row: P.
❋ Rep last 2 rows twice more. [14 sts]
❋ Work 10 rows in st st, beg with a K row.
❋ Next row: K2, k2tog, K6, ssk, K2. [12 sts]
❋ Next row: p2tog, P to last 2 sts, p2tog. [10 sts]
❋ Bind off.

BODY
The body is knitted from the lower edge to the neck edge and includes the corset.
Make 2 pieces
❋ Cast on 12 sts in pale pink.
❋ Work 8 rows in st st, beg with a K row.
❋ Next row: K2, k2tog, K4, ssk, K2. [10 sts]
❋ Next row: K.

* Work 6 rows in st st, beg with a K row.
* Next row: K2, m1, K6, m1, K2. [12 sts]
* Work 3 rows in st st, beg with a P row.
* Break pale pink yarn and join flesh yarn.
* Work 2 rows in st st, beg with a K row.
* Next row: Bind off 1 st, K to end. [11 sts]
* Next row: Bind off 1 st pwise, P to end. [10 sts]
* Bind off.

LEGS
The feet and legs are knitted as one piece, starting at the sole of the foot.
Make 2
* Cast on 24 sts in flesh.
* Work 4 rows in st st, beg with a K row.
* Next row: K5, bind off 14 sts, K to end. [10 sts]
* Work 21 rows in st st, beg with a P row.
* Bind off.

ARMS
The arms are knitted from the top of the shoulder to the tip of the hand.
Make 2
* Cast on 9 sts in flesh.
* Work 18 rows in st st, beg with a K row.
* Next row: K2, k2tog, K1, ssk, K2. [7 sts]
* Next row: p2tog, P3, p2tog. [5 sts]
* Next row: k2tog, K1, ssk. [3 sts]
* Break yarn and thread through rem sts.

HAIR
* Work five 6½-in. (16-cm) crochet chains in pale gray.

MAKING UP
Place the two head pieces right sides together and whipstitch around the edges, leaving the top of the head open for turning and stuffing. Turn the head right side out, stuff, and close the gap using mattress stitch. Sew the body together using mattress stitch, leaving the lower edge open for turning and stuffing. Stuff and close the gap. Sew the head to the body.

Fold one leg in half lengthwise, right sides together, and whipstitch the top and lower edge of the foot. Turn the leg right side out and sew the back seam using mattress stitch. Repeat with the second leg. Stuff the legs and feet.

Fold one arm in half lengthwise, right sides together, and whipstitch around the hand. Turn the hand right side out and sew the long seam using mattress stitch. Repeat with the second arm. The arms do not need stuffing.

Sew the arms and legs in place.

Arrange the crochet chains for the hair on the head and sew in place.

Work two French knots in black yarn for the eyes. Work a circle of chain stitch around each eye using white yarn. Using flesh yarn, work a flattened coil of chain stitches for the nose and a straight stitch above each eye for the eyelids.

Using deep pink yarn, work two straight stitches side by side for the mouth, so that they form a flattened V shape. Add color to the cheeks and across the nose using a red colored pencil.

NIGHTGOWN
Make 2 pieces
* Cast on 18 sts in pale turquoise.
* 1st row: K1, (yo, k2tog) to last st, K1. [18 sts]
* Next row: P.
* Rep last 2 rows once more.
* Next row: K1, (yo, k2tog) to last st, K1. [18 sts]
* Next row: K.
* Work 20 rows in st st, beg with a K row.
* Next row: k2tog, (yo, k2tog) to last 2 sts, ssk. [16 sts]
* Next row: p2tog, P to last 2 sts, p2tog. [14 sts]
* Next row: K2, k2tog, K to last 4 sts, ssk, K2. [12 sts]
* Work 7 rows in st st, beg with a P row.
* K 2 rows.
* Bind off pwise.

TIE
Make 1
* Using pale pink yarn, work an 8½-in. (21-cm) crochet chain. Trim and fray the ends.

MAKING UP
Whipstitch ¼ in. (5 mm) at each side of the bound-off edge to form the neck hole. Join the side seams using mattress stitch, leaving the top 1 in. (2.5 cm) open to form the armholes. Thread the tie through the eyelets at the waist and fasten in a knot at the side.

SLIPPERS
Make 2
* Using size U.S. 2 (2.75 mm) needles, cast on 8 sts in pale pink.
* 1st row: inc1, K to last 2 sts, inc1, K1. [10 sts]
* Next row: P.
* Rep last 2 rows once more. [12 sts]
* Work 2 rows in st st, beg with a K row.
* Next row: inc1, K to last 2 sts, inc1, K1. [14 sts]
* Next row: P5, bind off 4 sts pwise, P to end. Turn work and cont on only these last 5 sts, leaving rem sts on needle or on a safety pin.
* Work 6 rows in st st, beg with a K row.
* Bind off.
* With rs facing, rejoin yarn to rem sts.
* Work 6 rows in st st, beg with a K row.
* Bind off.

BOWS
Make 2
* Work a 2½-in. (6-cm) crochet chain in white.

MAKING UP
Fold the slipper pieces in half lengthwise with the right side facing inward. Whipstitch the back and lower seams. Turn the right way out. Put the slippers on the doll and secure with a couple of stitches. Arrange the bows in figure-eight shapes with the yarn tails at the center, and use these tails to sew the bows in place.

BED JACKET
The main part of the bed jacket is knitted as one piece from the neck edge downward.
Make 1
* Cast on 26 sts in pale yellow.
* K 2 rows.

* Next row: K2, P4. Turn and work on only these 6 sts, leaving rem sts on needle.
* Next row: K.
* Next row: K2, P4.
* Rep these last 2 rows once more. Break yarn and join it to rem sts on ws of work.
* Next row: P14. Turn and work on only these 14 sts, leaving rem sts on needle.
* Work 4 rows in st st, beg with a K row. Break yarn and join it to rem 6 sts on ws of work.
* Next row: P4, K2.
* Next row: K.
* Rep last 2 rows once more.
* Next row: P4, K2.
* Next row: K across all 26 sts.
* Next row: K2, P to last 2 sts, K2.
* Next row: K8, m1, K10, m1, K8. [28 sts]
* Next row: K2, P to last 2 sts, K2.
* Next row: K8, m1, K12, m1, K8. [30 sts]
* Next row: K2, (yo, k2tog) to last 2 sts, K2. [30 sts]
* K 2 rows.
* Bind off loosely.

SLEEVES

The sleeves are knitted from the armhole edge to the cuff.
Make 2
* Cast on 12 sts in pale yellow.
* Work 11 rows in st st, beg with a K row.
* K 2 rows.
* Bind off.

MAKING UP

Sew the sleeve seems using mattress stitch and whipstitch the sleeves in place around the armholes from the inside of the jacket.

PANTIES

The panties are knitted as one piece.
Make 1
* Cast on 16 sts in pale pink for first leg.
* K 2 rows.
* Work 3 rows in st st, beg with a P row.
* Break yarn and leave sts on a stitch holder or spare needle.
* Work second leg in the same way, but do not break yarn.
* Next row: K 16 sts from leg just knitted then 16 sts from first leg. [32 sts]
* Next row: P.
* Next row: K8, m1, K16, m1, K8. [34 sts]
* Next row: P.
* Next row: K8, m1, K1, m1, K16, m1, K1, m1, K8. [38 sts]
* Work 7 rows in st st, beg with a P row.
* Next row: K2, (yo, k2tog) to last 2 sts, K2. [38 sts]
* K 2 rows.
* Bind off loosely.

MAKING UP

Fold the two sides inward to create the basic panties shape. Sew the inside leg seams and the back seam using mattress stitch. For the cord, work an 8-in. (20-cm) crochet chain in white. Thread the cord through the eyelets at the waist edge.

HAT

Make 2 pieces
* Cast on 18 sts in white.
* Work 3 rows in st st, beg with a P row.
* Next row: K1, (yo, k2tog) to last st, K1. [18 sts]
* K 2 rows.
* Next row: P.
* Next row: K.
* Next row: p2tog, P to last 2 sts, p2tog. [16 sts]
* Next row: K1, (k2tog) twice, K to last 5 sts, (ssk) twice, K1. [12 sts]
* Next row: p2tog, P to last 2 sts, p2tog. [10 sts]
* Bind off.

MAKING UP

With the hat pieces right sides together, whipstitch around the sides and top. Work a 3¼-in. (8-cm) crochet chain in pale turquoise yarn, tie it in a bow, and fasten it to the front of the hat.

HOW TO KNIT
The Wolf

He may be knitted in a gorgeous soft gray yarn, but this wolf is one tricky and deceitful creature. With his sly smile, he's all friendly and sweet-talking one minute, but baring his teeth and determined to grab himself a decent meal the next minute. Use him again in the story of the Three Little Pigs.

DOLL

HEAD

The head is knitted from the back to the front.
Make 2 pieces
❋ Cast on 15 sts in gray.
❋ Work 8 rows in st st, beg with a K row.
❋ Next row: K2, m1, K11, m1, K2. [17 sts]
❋ Work 3 rows in st st, beg with a P row.
❋ Next row; K2, k2tog, K to last 4 sts, ssk, K2. [15 sts]
❋ Next row: P.
❋ Rep last 2 rows 4 times more. [7 sts]
❋ Next row: K1, k2tog, K1, ssk, K1. [5 sts]
❋ Next row: P.
❋ Next row: k2tog, K1, ssk. [3 sts]
❋ Next row: s1, p2tog, psso. [1 st]
❋ Break yarn and pull it through rem st.

EARS

Make 2
❋ Using size U.S. 2 (2.75 mm) needles, cast on 6 sts in gray.
❋ K 6 rows.
❋ Next row: k2tog, K2, ssk. [4 sts]
❋ K 2 rows.
❋ Next row: k2tog, ssk. [2 sts]
❋ Next row: k2tog. Break yarn and pull it through rem st.

BODY

The body is knitted from the bottom edge upward.
Make 2 pieces
❋ Cast on 14 sts in gray.
❋ Work 6 rows in st st, beg with a K row.
❋ Next row: K2, m1, K to last 2 sts, m1, K2. [16 sts]
❋ Next row: P.
❋ Rep last 2 rows 3 times more. [22 sts]

❋ Work 10 rows in st st, beg with a P row.
❋ Next row: K2, k2tog, K to last 4 sts, ssk, K2. [20 sts]
❋ Work 3 rows in st st, beg with a P row.
❋ Next row: K2, k2tog, K to last 4 sts, ssk, K2. [18 sts]
❋ Next row: P.
❋ Rep last 2 rows 4 more times. [10 sts]
❋ Work 4 rows in st st, beg with a K row.
❋ Bind off.

LEGS

The feet and legs are knitted in one piece, starting at the sole of the foot.
Make 2
❋ Cast on 30 sts in gray.
❋ Work 4 rows in st st, beg with a K row.
❋ Next row: K4, bind off 22 sts, K4. [8 sts]
❋ Work 9 rows in st st, beg with a P row.
❋ Bind off.

ARMS

The arms are knitted from the shoulder to the paw.
Make 2
❋ Cast on 8 sts in gray.
❋ Work 16 rows in st st, beg with a K row.
❋ Next row: K1, k2tog, K2, ssk, K1. [6 sts]
❋ Next row: p2tog, P2, p2tog. [4 sts]
❋ Bind off.

MAKING UP

With the two head pieces wrong sides together, sew the sides using mattress stitch, leaving the back edge open for stuffing. Stuff the head and close the gap using mattress stitch. With the two body pieces wrong sides together, sew the sides and lower edge using mattress stitch. Stuff the body through the neck edge. Position the head on the neck so that the neck forms a circle on the underside of the head and sew it in place.

Fold one leg in half in half lengthwise, right sides together, and whipstitch the top and bottom of the foot. Turn the leg right side out and sew the back seam using mattress stitch. Repeat with the second leg. Stuff and sew in place.

Fold one arm in half lengthwise, right sides together, and whipstitch around the paw. Turn the arm right side out and sew the long seam using mattress stitch. Repeat with the second arm. The arms do not need stuffing. Sew the arms in place.

Sew the ears in place, curving them slightly at the bottom.

Work two French knots in black yarn for the eyes. Work two circles of chain stitch around each eye using white yarn. Work a small coil of chain stitch in black yarn for the nose. Work a row of chain stitch in medium pink yarn for the mouth and work a row of running stitch over the chain stitch in white yarn for the teeth.

Rapunzel

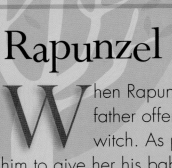

When Rapunzel was just a tiny baby, her father offended Dame Gothel, a powerful witch. As punishment, the Dame forced him to give her his baby daughter. She kept the little girl under lock and key. Rapunzel saw nothing of the outside world, and she didn't meet anyone except for the witch. As she got older, she grew beautiful and accomplished, with golden hair that was amazingly long and shiny. In her own way, the wicked Dame Gothel loved the girl and was always afraid that her prize might escape, so she locked Rapunzel up in a tall tower that didn't even have a staircase or a door.

As before, Rapunzel saw no one but Dame Gothel. When the Dame arrived at the tower, she would call up to its window, saying, **"Rapunzel, Rapunzel, let down your hair!"** and the girl would hang her heavy golden braid out of the window for the witch to crawl up. Hand over hand, the Dame would laboriously climb up Rapunzel's hair, hauling with her a basket of food and other things—books and sewing materials—with which she expected the girl to fill the long hours until her next visit.

The tower looked out onto a lonely landscape and few people passed by. One day, however, a prince came down the deserted road (he'd been out hunting and had lost his way). The tower intrigued him, and as he approached, he heard a girl's voice, singing sweetly, coming through the window. Walking around the tower's bottom he could not find a door, so he called up to the window. **"Who's singing? Do you live there? Lean out so that I can see your face!"** So Rapunzel leaned from the window and, for the first time, saw a man (and a handsome one at that).

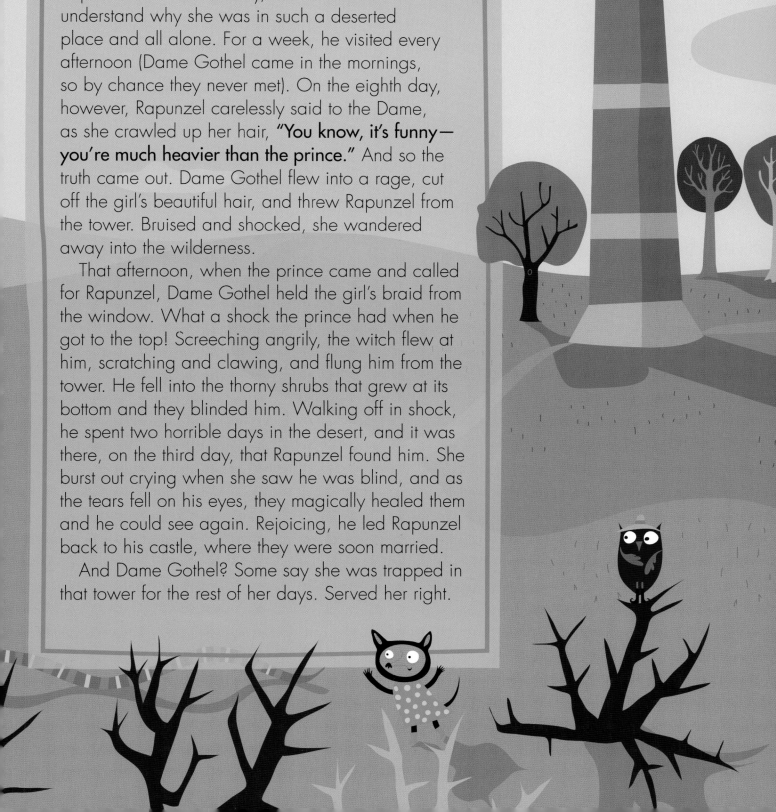

Rapunzel was immediately intrigued; when the prince asked how he could talk to her, she let down her hair and told him to climb up it, and he eagerly did so. The prince was entranced by Rapunzel's wit and beauty, but he couldn't understand why she was in such a deserted place and all alone. For a week, he visited every afternoon (Dame Gothel came in the mornings, so by chance they never met). On the eighth day, however, Rapunzel carelessly said to the Dame, as she crawled up her hair, **"You know, it's funny—you're much heavier than the prince."** And so the truth came out. Dame Gothel flew into a rage, cut off the girl's beautiful hair, and threw Rapunzel from the tower. Bruised and shocked, she wandered away into the wilderness.

That afternoon, when the prince came and called for Rapunzel, Dame Gothel held the girl's braid from the window. What a shock the prince had when he got to the top! Screeching angrily, the witch flew at him, scratching and clawing, and flung him from the tower. He fell into the thorny shrubs that grew at its bottom and they blinded him. Walking off in shock, he spent two horrible days in the desert, and it was there, on the third day, that Rapunzel found him. She burst out crying when she saw he was blind, and as the tears fell on his eyes, they magically healed them and he could see again. Rejoicing, he led Rapunzel back to his castle, where they were soon married.

And Dame Gothel? Some say she was trapped in that tower for the rest of her days. Served her right.

Rapunzel

Blessed with an enchanting voice, not to mention those flowing blonde locks, Rapunzel seems to have it all. But her sad and lonely childhood tells a different story. So when a prince heard her singing, how could she resist his attention? Knitted here in shades of pink and lilac, Rapunzel has a long braid that can hang down or be wound around her head in a traditional European style.

MATERIALS
⅟₁₆ oz./2 g (5½ yd./5 m) white DK yarn
⅜ oz./11 g (30 yd./27 m) flesh DK yarn
⅛ oz./3 g (8 yd./7 m) deep pink DK yarn
¼ oz./5 g (13 yd./12 m) light ocher DK yarn
⅟₁₆ oz./2 g (5½ yd./5 m) lilac DK yarn
⅟₁₆ oz./2 g (5½ yd./5 m) silver crochet yarn
A small amount of black DK yarn
A very small amount of red DK yarn
One medium size deep pink button
Two ⅜-in./10-mm silver star sequins
White sewing thread
⅜–½ oz./10–15 g polyester toy filling
Red colored pencil

Use size U.S. 2/3 (3 mm) knitting needles
except when instructed to use size U.S. 2
(2.75 mm) knitting needles.

DOLL

HEAD AND BODY
The head and body are knitted together from the bottom of the body upward and include the underpants and top.

Front
Make 1
※ Cast on 14 sts in white.
※ Work 7 rows in st st, beg with a K row.
※ Next row: K.
※ Break white yarn and join deep pink yarn.
※ Work 13 rows in st st, beg with a K row.
※ Next row: K.
※ Break deep pink yarn and join flesh yarn.
※ Next row: K.
※ Next row: (p2tog) twice, P to last 4 sts, (p2tog) twice. [10 sts]
※ Next row: K2, inc1 into next 5 sts, K3. [15 sts]
※ Next row: P.
※ Next row: K1, inc1, K to last 3 sts, inc1, K2. [17 sts]
※ Next row: P. *
※ Rep last 2 rows 3 times more. [23 sts]
※ Work 2 rows in st st, beg with a K row.

* Next row: K2, (k2tog) twice, K11, (ssk) twice, K2. [19 sts]
* Next row: p2tog, P to last 2 sts, p2tog. [17 sts]
* Next row: K2, (k2tog) twice, K5, (ssk) twice, K2. [13 sts]
* Next row: p2tog, P to last 2 sts, p2tog. [11 sts]
* Bind off.

Back

Make 1

* Work as for front to *.
* Next row: K1, inc1, K to last 3 sts, inc1, K1. [19 sts]
* Next row: P.
* Break flesh yarn and join light ocher yarn.
* Next row: K1, inc1, K to last 3 sts, inc1, K1. [21 sts]
* Next row: P.
* Rep last 2 rows once more. [23 sts]
* Work 2 rows in st st, beg with a K row.
* Next row: K2, (k2tog) twice, K11, (ssk) twice, K2. [19 sts]
* Next row: p2tog, P to last 2 sts, p2tog. [17 sts]
* Next row: K2, (k2tog) twice, K5, (ssk) twice, K2. [13 sts]
* Next row: p2tog, P to last 2 sts, p2tog. [11 sts]
* Bind off.

LEGS

The feet and legs are knitted as one piece, starting at the sole of the foot.

Make 2

* Cast on 22 sts in flesh.
* Work 4 rows in st st, beg with a K row.
* Next row: K5, bind off 12 sts, K5. [10 sts]
* Work 19 rows in st st, beg with a K row.
* Bind off.

ARMS

The arms are knitted from the shoulder to the hand.

Make 2

* Cast on 9 sts in lilac.
* 1st row: K1, inc1, K to last 3 sts, inc1, K2. [11 sts]
* Next row: P.
* Next row: K2, m1, K to last 2 sts, m1, K1. [13 sts]

* Work 3 rows in st st, beg with a P row.
* Next row: K2, k2tog, K5, ssk, K2. [11 sts]
* Next row: p2tog, P to last 2 sts, p2tog. [9 sts]
* Next row: K2, k2tog, K1, ssk, K2. [7 sts]
* Next row: K.
* Break lilac yarn and join flesh yarn.
* Work 10 rows in st st, beg with a K row.
* Next row: K1, k2tog, K1, ssk, K1. [5 sts]
* Next row: p2tog, P1, p2tog. [3 sts]
* Next row: s1, k2tog, psso. [1 st]
* Break yarn and pull it through rem st.

MAKING UP

With the two head and body pieces right sides together, whipstitch around the head. Turn the piece right side out and sew the side seams of the body using mattress stitch, leaving the lower edge open for stuffing. Stuff the doll and close the gap using mattress stitch.

Fold the legs in half lengthwise, right sides together, and whipstitch the top and lower edge of the feet. Turn right sides out, sew the back seam using mattress stitch, and stuff.

Fold the arms in half lengthwise, right sides together, and whipstitch around the hand. Turn right sides out and sew the long seam using mattress stitch. Stuff the top part of the arms lightly.

Sew the arms and legs in place.

Using light ocher yarn, work a few rows of chain stitch at the front of the head for the hair. For the braid, cut twelve 40-in. (1-m) lengths of light ocher yarn. Join the centers of the yarn lengths to the left side of the doll's face. Braid the yarn to the ends and secure.

Work two French knots in black yarn for the eyes. Work two circles of chain stitch around each eye using white yarn. Using a separated ply of black yarn, work five straight stitches above each eye for eyelashes. Work two short rows of chain stitch in flesh yarn for the nose.

Work a V shape for the mouth in red yarn.

Using silver crochet thread, sew the two star sequins in position for earrings. Add color to the cheeks using a red colored pencil.

SKIRT OF DRESS

Make 2 pieces

* Cast on 22 sts in lilac.
* 1st row: K1, (yo, k2tog) to last st, K1.
* Work 5 rows in st st, beg with a P row.
* Leave lilac yarn at side and join deep pink yarn.
* K 2 rows.
* Break deep pink yarn and work remainder of skirt in lilac.
* Work 2 rows in st st, beg with a K row.
* Next row: K2, k2tog, K to last 4 sts, ssk, K2. [20 sts]
* Work 3 rows in st st, beg with a P row.
* Rep last 4 rows 3 times more. [14 sts]
* Work 2 rows in st st, beg with a K row.
* Bind off pwise.

MAKING UP

Join the side seams of using mattress stitch. Whipstitch the waist in place. Sew the button in position at the neck.

SHOES

Make 2

* Using size U.S. 2 (2.75 mm) needles, cast on 8 sts in silver crochet yarn.
* 1st row: inc1, K to last 2 sts, inc1, K1. [10 sts]
* Next row: P.
* Rep last 2 rows once more. [12 sts]
* Work 2 rows in st st, beg with a K row.
* Next row: inc1, K to last 2 sts, inc1, K1. [14 sts]
* Next row: P5, bind off 4 sts pwise, P to end. Turn work and cont on only these last 5 sts, leaving rem sts on needle or on a safety pin.
* Work 6 rows in st st, beg with a K row.
* Bind off.
* With rs facing, rejoin yarn to rem sts.
* Work 6 rows in st st, beg with a K row.
* Bind off.

MAKING UP

Fold the shoe pieces in half lengthwise with the right side facing inward. Whipstitch the back and lower seam of the shoes. Turn the right way out. Put the shoes on the doll and secure with a couple of stitches. Work a couple of large straight stitches across the foot in a cross shape.

HOW TO KNIT
Dame Gothel

Mean-spirited, ugly, jealous, vindictive . . . I could go on. Dame Gothel is a very nasty piece of work. But in the world of make-believe, we know that characters like the dame normally get their comeuppance. With her wild, black hair and clothes that she thinks make her look gorgeous, Dame Gothel is every inch the perfect fairy-tale villain.

MATERIALS
¼ oz./7.5 g (20 yd./18 m) flesh DK yarn
¹⁄₁₆ oz./2 g (5 yd./4.5 m) pale pink DK yarn
¹⁄₁₆ oz./2.5 g (7 yd./6 m) medium brown DK yarn
⅛ oz./3 g (8½ yd./7.5 m) dark purple DK yarn
⅛ oz./3.5 g (9 yd./8 m) black mohair yarn
⅛ oz./4.5 g (12 yd./11 m) aqua DK yarn
⅛ oz./4 g (10½ yd./9.5 m) medium pink DK yarn
½ oz./12 g (33 yd./30 m) teal DK yarn
Very small amounts of white, black,
bright red, and camel DK yarns
One small turquoise button
One snap fastener
Sewing thread

Use size U.S. 2/3 (3 mm) knitting needles
except when instructed to use size U.S. 2
(2.75 mm) or U.S. 5 (3.75 mm) knitting needles.

DOLL

HEAD

The head is knitted from the bottom of the chin to the top of the forehead.

Make 2 pieces

❉ Cast on 4 sts in flesh.

❉ 1st row: (inc1, K1) twice. [6 sts]

❉ Next row: P.

❉ Next row: K1, m1, K to last st, m1, K1. [8 sts]

❉ Next row: P.

❉ Rep last 2 rows 3 times more. [14 sts]

❉ Work 10 rows in st st, beg with a K row.

❉ Next row: K2, k2tog, K6, ssk, K2. [12 sts]

❉ Next row: p2tog, P to last 2 sts, p2tog. [10 sts]

❉ Bind off.

NOSE

Make 1

❉ Cast on 6 sts in flesh.

❉ Work 2 rows in st st, beg with a K row.

❉ Next row: k2tog, K2, ssk. [4 sts]

❉ Work 3 rows in st st, beg with a P row.

❉ Next row: k2tog, ssk. [2 sts]

❉ Work 3 rows in st st, beg with a P row.

❉ Next row: k2tog. Break yarn and pull through rem st.

BODY

The body is knitted from the lower edge to the neck edge.

Make 2 pieces

❉ Cast on 12 sts in pale pink.

❉ Work 8 rows in st st, beg with a K row.

❉ Next row: K2, k2tog, K4, ssk, K2. [10 sts]

❉ Next row: K.

❉ Break pale pink yarn and join medium brown yarn.

❉ Work 6 rows in st st, beg with a K row.

❉ Next row: K2, m1, K6, m1, K2. [12 sts]

❉ Work 7 rows in st st, beg with a P row.

❉ Next row; Bind off 1 st, K to end. [11 sts]

❉ Next row: Bind off 1 st pwise, P to end. [10 sts]

❉ Bind off.

LEGS

The boots and legs are knitted as one piece, starting at the sole of the foot.

Make 2

❉ Cast on 26 sts in dark purple.

❉ Work 4 rows in st st, beg with a K row.

❉ Next row: K5, bind off 16 sts, K to end. [10 sts]

❉ Work 8 rows in st st, beg with a P row.

❉ K 3 rows.

❉ Break dark purple yarn and join flesh yarn.

❉ Work 12 rows in st st, beg with a K row.

❉ Bind off.

ARMS

The arms are knitted from the top of the shoulder to the tip of the hand.

Make 2

❉ Cast on 9 sts in medium brown.

❉ Work 13 rows in st st, beg with a K row.

❉ Next row: K.

❉ Break medium brown yarn and join flesh yarn.

❉ Work 4 rows in st st, beg with a K row.

❉ Next row: K2, k2tog, K1, ssk, K2. [7 sts]

❉ Next row: p2tog, P3, p2tog. [5 sts]

❉ Next row: k2tog, K1, ssk. [3 sts]

❉ Break yarn and thread through rem sts.

MAKING UP

Place the two head pieces right sides together and whipstitch around the edges, leaving the top of the head open for turning and stuffing. Turn the head right side out, stuff, and close the gap using mattress stitch. Sew the body together using mattress stitch, leaving the lower edge open for turning and stuffing. Stuff and close the gap. Sew the head to the body.

Fold one leg in half lengthwise, right sides together, and whipstitch the top and lower edge of the boot. Turn the leg right side out and sew the back seam using mattress stitch. Repeat for the second leg. Stuff the legs and boots.

Fold one arm in half lengthwise, right sides together, and whipstitch around the hand. Turn the arm right side out and sew the long seam using mattress stitch. Repeat with the second arm. The arms do not need stuffing.

Sew the arms and legs in place.

Cut the black mohair yarn into 10-in. (25-cm) lengths and gather together in a bunch. Secure the center of the lengths to the top of the head and at each side of the face. Trim the lengths if necessary.

Work two French knots in black yarn for the eyes. Work a circle of chain stitch around each eye using white yarn. Fold the nose piece in half lengthwise and whipstitch in position. Using camel yarn, work a few French knots on the face to represent warts.

Divide a short length of bright red yarn into two thinner strands. Work two straight stitches at an angle, one over the top of the other, for the mouth.

DRESS

Make 2 pieces

❋ Using size U.S. 5 (3.75 mm) needles, cast on 16 sts in aqua.
❋ 1st row: P.
❋ Next row: K1, (yo, k2tog) to last st, K1.
❋ Work 13 rows in st st, beg with a P row.
❋ Break aqua yarn and join medium pink yarn.
❋ K 2 rows.
❋ Next row: K1, k2tog, K to last 3 sts, ssk, K1. [14 sts]
❋ Work 3 rows in st st, beg with a P row.
❋ Rep last 4 rows once more. [12 sts]
❋ Next row: Bind off 2 sts, K2 (3 sts on needle after binding off), bind off 2 sts, K to end. [8 sts]
❋ Turn and work on only 5 sts just knitted, keeping other sts on needle.
❋ Next row: Bind off 2 sts pwise, P to end. [3 sts]
❋ Next row: k2tog, K1. [2 sts]

❋ Work 3 rows in st st, beg with a P row.
❋ Next row: k2tog. [1 st]
❋ Break yarn and pull it through rem st.
❋ With ws facing, rejoin yarn to rem sts on needle.
❋ Next row: p2tog, P1. [2 sts]
❋ Work 3 rows in st st, beg with a K row.
❋ Next row: p2tog. [1 st]
❋ Break yarn and pull it through rem st.

MAKING UP

With wrong sides together, join the side seams of the dress using mattress stitch and matching yarns. Join the front to the back at the shoulders.

COAT

The coat is knitted in one piece from the neck edge downward.

Make 1

❋ Cast on 28 sts in teal.
❋ K 2 rows.
❋ Next row: K2, P5, K1. Turn work and cont on these 8 sts only, leaving rem sts on needle.
❋ Next row: K.
❋ Next row: K2, P5, K1.
❋ Rep these 2 rows 3 times more.
❋ Break yarn and join it to rem sts on ws of work.
❋ Next row: K1, P10, K1. Turn work and cont on these 12 sts only, leaving rem sts on needle.
❋ Next row: K.
❋ Next row: K1, P10, K1.
❋ Rep these 2 rows 3 times more.
❋ Break yarn and join it to rem 8 sts on ws of work.

❋ Next row: K1, P5, K2.
❋ Next row: K.
❋ Rep last 2 rows 3 times more.
❋ Next row: K1, P5, K2.
❋ Now work across all 28 sts.
❋ Next row: K.
❋ Next row: K2, P to last 2 sts, K2.
❋ Next row: K6, m1, K4, m1, K8, m1, K4, m1, K6. [32 sts]
❋ Next row: K2, P to last 2 sts, K2.
❋ Next row: K.
❋ Next row: K2, P to last 2 sts, K2.
❋ Next row: K7, m1, K4, m1, K10, m1, K4, m1, K7. [36 sts]
❋ Next row: K2, P to last 2 sts, K2.
❋ Next row: (K2, m1) to last 2 sts, K2. [53 sts]
❋ Next row: K2, P to last 2 sts, K2.
❋ Next row: K.
❋ Rep last 2 rows 10 times more.
❋ K 4 rows.
❋ Bind off.

MAKING UP

Sew the button to the right side of the coat. Sew the top of the snap fastener under the button and the bottom of the snap fastener on the corresponding part of the other side of the coat.

Rapunzel's Prince

Handsome, gallant, love-struck—and also a prince. It's not hard to see why Rapunzel found this young man so attractive. Wearing a fashionable red jacket and boots suitable for a lot of walking through the woods, he was prepared to go to the ends of the earth for her, whatever obstacles were put in his way. We're sure that you'll fall in love with this prince, too.

MATERIALS

⅜ oz./11 g (30 yd./27 m) beige DK yarn

1/16 oz./1.5 g (3½ yd./3 m) black DK yarn

⅜ oz./9 g (24 yd./22 m) red DK yarn

¼ oz./6.5 g (17½ yd./16 m) chestnut brown DK yarn

¼ oz./8 g (21 yd./19 m) caramel DK yarn

Small amount of deep yellow DK yarn

Very small amounts of white and dark red DK yarns

Very small amount of gold crochet yarn

Three ⅛-in./4-mm gold beads

Sewing thread

⅜–½ oz./10–15 g polyester toy filling

Red colored pencil

Use size U.S. 2/3 (3 mm) knitting needles except when instructed to use size U.S. 2 (2.75 mm) knitting needles.

DOLL

HEAD
Front
Make 1
* Cast on 12 sts in beige.
* 1st row: K1, inc1, K to last 3 sts, inc1, K2. [14 sts]
* Next row: P.
* Next row: K2, m1, K to last 2 sts, m1, K2. [16 sts]*
* Work 13 rows in st st, beg with a P row.
* Next row: K2, k2tog, K to last 4 sts, ssk, K2. [14 sts]
* Next row: p2tog, P to last 2 sts, p2tog. [12 sts]
* Rep last 2 rows once more. [8 sts]
* Bind off.

Back
Make 1
* Work as for front to *.
* Work 11 rows in st st, beg with a P row.
* Break beige yarn and join black yarn.
* Work 2 rows in st st, beg with a K row.
* Next row: K2, k2tog, K to last 4 sts, ssk, K2. [14 sts]
* Next row: p2tog, P to last 2 sts, p2tog. [12 sts]
* Rep last 2 rows once more. [8 sts]
* Bind off.

EARS
Make 2
* Using size U.S. 2 (2.75 mm) needles, cast on 4 sts in beige.
* 1st row: (k2tog) twice. [2 sts]
* Next row: p2tog.
* Break yarn and pull it through rem st.

BODY
Make 2 pieces
* Cast on 14 sts in beige.
* Work 20 rows in st st, beg with a K row.
* Next row: Bind off 1 st, K to end. [13 sts]
* Next row: Bind off 1 st pwise, P to end. [12 sts]
* Bind off.

LEGS
The feet and legs are knitted in one piece, starting at the sole of the foot.
Make 2
* Cast on 26 sts in beige.
* Work 4 rows in st st, beg with a K row.
* Next row: K6, bind off 14 sts, K to end. [12 sts]
* Work 25 rows in st st, beg with a P row.
* Bind off.

ARMS
The arms are knitted from the shoulder to the hand.
Make 2
* Cast on 10 sts in red.
* Work 18 rows in st st, beg with a K row.
* Leave red yarn at the side and join deep yellow yarn.
* K 2 rows. Break deep yellow yarn.
* K 2 rows in red yarn.
* Break red yarn and join beige yarn.
* Work 2 rows in st st, beg with a K row.
* Next row: K2, k2tog, K2, ssk, K2. [8 sts]
* Next row: p2tog, P to last 2 sts, p2tog. [6 sts]
* Bind off.

MAKING UP
Place the two head pieces right sides together and whipstitch around the edges, leaving the top of the head open for turning and stuffing. Turn the head right side out, stuff, and close the gap using mattress stitch. Sew the ears in place. Sew the body together using mattress stitch, leaving the lower edge open for turning and stuffing. Stuff and close the gap. Sew the head to the body.

Fold one leg in half lengthwise, right sides together, and whipstitch the top and lower edge of the feet. Turn the leg right side out and sew the back seam using mattress stitch. Repeat for the second leg. Stuff the legs and feet.

Fold one arm in half lengthwise, right sides together, and whipstitch around the hand. Turn the arm right side out and sew the long seam using mattress stitch. Repeat for the second arm. The arms do not need stuffing.

Sew the arms and legs in place.

Using black yarn, work a few rows of chain stitch at the front of the head for the hair, using the photograph as a guide (see page 35).

Work two French knots in black yarn for the eyes. Work two circles of chain stitch around each eye, using white yarn. Work two short rows of chain stitch in flesh yarn for the nose.

Using dark red yarn, work two straight stitches side by side for the mouth, so that they form a flattened V shape. Add color to he cheeks using a red colored pencil.

JACKET FRONT AND BACK
The two front sides and the back of the jacket are knitted as one piece, from the lower edge to the neck edge. The sleeves have been knitted as part of the doll.
Make 1
* Cast on 30 sts in red.
* K 2 rows.
* Next and every ws row: K2, P to last 2 sts, K2.
* Work 20 rows in st st, beg with a K row, remembering to K2 sts at beg and end of every ws row.
* Next row: K8, turn, and work on only these sts, leaving rem sts on needle.
* Next row: P6, K2.
* Next row: K.
* Next row: P6, K2.
* Rep last 2 rows once more.
* Next row: K.
* Break yarn and leave sts on needle.
* On rs of work, join yarn to rem sts.
* Next row: K14.
* Turn and work on only these 14 sts.
* Work 6 rows in st st, beg with a P row.
* Break yarn and transfer sts onto right-hand needle without knitting them.
* On rs of work, join yarn to rem 8 sts on left-hand needle.
* Next row: K.
* Next row: K2, P6.
* Next row: K.
* Rep last 2 rows twice more.
* Now knit across all 30 sts on needle.

- Next row: Bind off 2 sts kwise, P7 [8 sts on needle, including rem st from binding off], (p2tog) twice, P2, (p2tog) twice, P to last 2 sts, K2. [24 sts]
- Next row: Bind off 2 sts, K to end. [22 sts]
- K 2 rows.
- Bind off.

BELT

Make 1

- Cast on 30 sts in chestnut brown.
- Work 2 rows in st st, beg with a K row.
- Bind off pwise.

MAKING UP

Put the jacket on the doll and whipstitch the armhole edges around the top of the arms. Overlap the jacket fronts and sew the three gold beads in place on the right front of the jacket. Fasten the jacket by using the gaps between stitches on the left front for buttonholes. Whipstitch the short edges of the belt. Position on the doll. Using doubled gold crochet yarn, work a series of straight stitches to form a square to represent a buckle in the center of the belt.

PANTS

The pants are knitted as one piece.

Make 1

- Cast on 14 sts for first leg in caramel.
- K 2 rows.
- Work 23 rows in st st, beg with a P row.
- Break yarn and leave sts on spare needle.
- Work a second pants leg exactly as the first, but don't break yarn.
- Next row: K14 sts from second pants leg, then knit across 14 sts from first pants leg. [28 sts]
- Work 9 rows in st st, beg with a P row.
- Next row: (K1, P1) to end.
- Rep last row once more.
- Bind off loosely, keeping in K1, P1 pattern.

MAKING UP

Using mattress stitch, join the back seam so that the lowest part of the seam is level with the crotch. Join the two inside leg seams, again using mattress stitch.

BOOTS

Make 2

- Cast on 28 sts in chestnut brown.
- K 2 rows.
- Work 4 rows in st st, beg with a K row.
- Next row: K8, bind off 12 sts, K to end. [16 sts]
- Work 10 rows in st st, beg with a P row.
- Next row: K.
- Bind off pwise loosely.

MAKING UP

Fold the pieces in half widthwise, right sides together. Whipstitch the lower and upper seams of the foot. Turn the boots right side out and sew the back seams using mattress stitch.

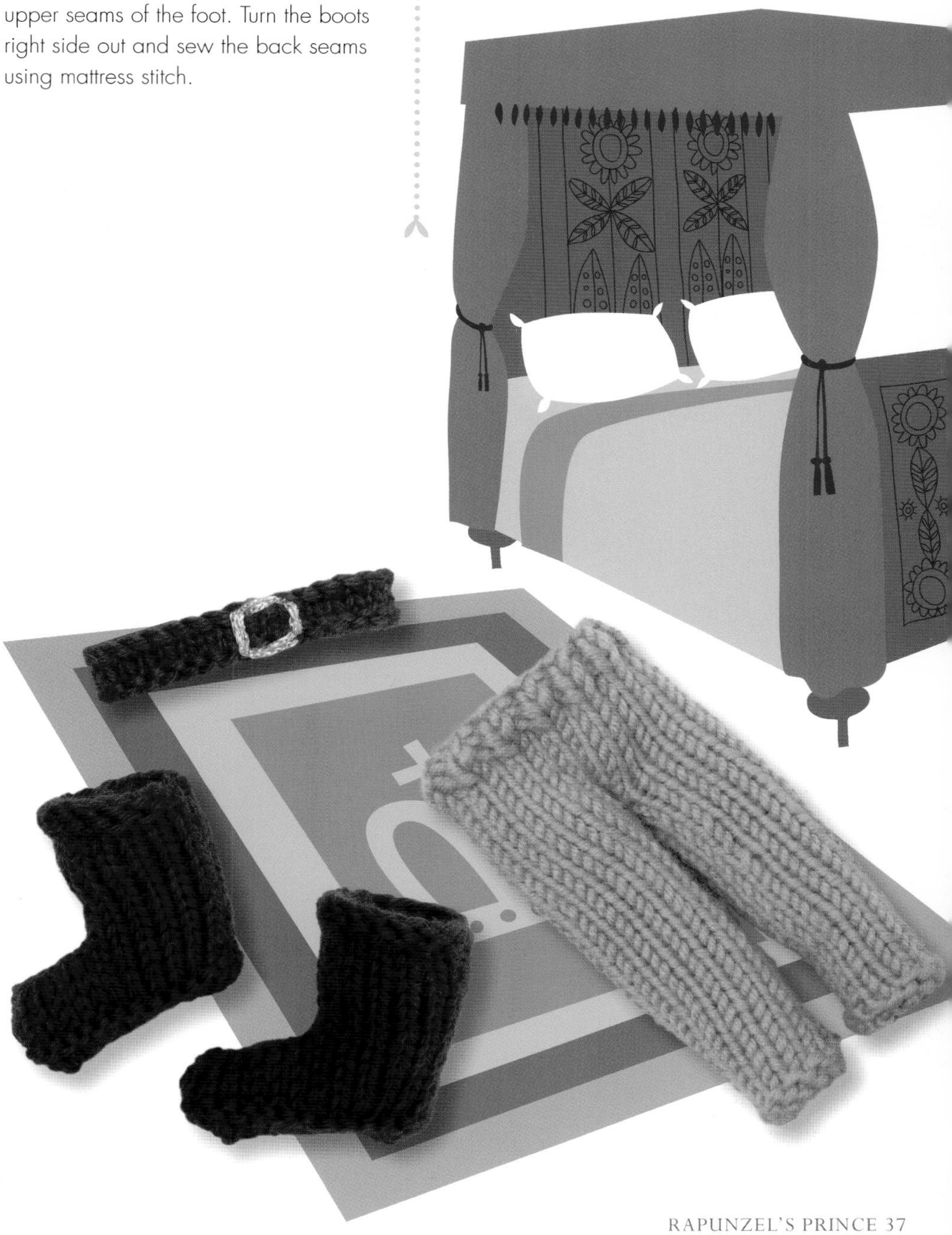

Hansel and Gretel

Hansel and Gretel were twins: bright, brave, and very close to one another. Sadly, their mother died when they were young, and when their father remarried he chose badly. Their new stepmother was very jealous of his children. Their father was a poor woodcutter and the stepmother constantly urged him to take the children miles into the wood and leave them there—**"We're too poor to feed them; it's kinder not to watch them starve . . ."** He gave in to her and took the children deep into the forest and left them there.

Hansel was no fool. He was suspicious about the long walk, and when their father disappeared, he showed Gretel that he had left a trail of little white pebbles to lead them back home. How angry the stepmother was when they trotted in the door! The very next day, she nagged the woodcutter into taking them for another long walk into the forest. This time Hansel had no pebbles, only a slice of bread. He left a trail of crumbs, but when his father disappeared again and he looked for them to follow, he found that the birds had eaten them up.

"Cheer up, Hansel," said his sister, who was also full of spirit. **"Let's walk on for a while and see what we can find."** And after two hours of walking, the twins arrived at a very peculiar and wonderful house.

The roof and the walls were made of gingerbread—not the dry, hard type, but the soft and delicious kind that's decorated with icing. Candy drops were set into the icing, and the windows were made from tasty-looking barley sugar and golden butterscotch. Both hungry twins broke off big chunks of cake and began to eat.

But . . . **"Who's munching on my house?"** came a shrill voice, and an old lady limped out of the house. The children stared—who would have thought that such a gorgeous house would belong to such a grubby creature? Seemingly friendly, she invited them in. Inside the house, however, it was a different story. True, the table was covered with cakes and other rich foods, but before they'd had time to look around properly, the witch (for so the old lady was) had roughly thrust Hansel into a large iron cage in the corner and turned the lock on him. **"Ha!"** she jeered.
"I'm sick of sweet things. I'm going to feed you every day and when you grow fat, I will turn you into a meaty stew. You," turning to Gretel, **"will do the housework."**

How scared they were! But they were resourceful, and they were sure they could find a way out before Hansel was eaten. The key to the cage was on a string around the witch's neck, and she kept a sharp eye on them. Every day, she fed Hansel sweet things and, because her eyesight was poor, asked to feel his finger so that she could tell how fat he was getting. Hansel stuck out a finger of barley sugar instead of his own, and the witch grew angry when he didn't put on weight. Finally, **"Heat up the oven,"** she told Gretel. **"I'm going to eat him anyway!"** Gretel saw her chance, sticking her head in the oven, she said, **"It seems very hot, but I can't really tell."** Huffing and puffing, the witch leaned into the oven. Quick as a flash, Gretel seized the string with the key with one hand and gave the witch a push with the other. The nasty old thing fell into the flames and was burned to death.

And the twins? Filling a bag with the witch's treasure, they ran through the forest until they found their way back to their father's house. When they arrived, they found that their stepmother had died while they were away. Their father cried with joy to have his children back. And they all lived together happily ever after.

HOW TO KNIT
Hansel

Hansel is a fashionable little guy. Dressed in a pair of striking emerald green shorts, red shirt, and royal blue stockings, he also has a deep brown hat that sets his outfit off with style. As you'll discover in the story, this guy is more than just a handsome face. He's also street smart—and really protective of his sister, Gretel.

HANSEL
MATERIALS
1/16 oz./2 g (4½ yd./4 m) white DK yarn

1/8 oz./4.5 g (12 yd./11 m) red DK yarn

1/16 oz./2.5 g (6 yd./5.5 m) flesh DK yarn

1/16 oz./1.5 g (3½ yd./3 m) medium yellow DK yarn

1/16 oz./2.5 g (6 yd./5.5 m) dark brown DK yarn

1/16 oz./2 g (5 yd./4.5 m) royal blue DK yarn

1/4 oz./5.5 g (14½ yd./13 m) emerald green DK yarn

Very small amounts of black and deep pink DK yarns

Two small white buttons

Red sewing thread

3/8—1/2 oz./10—15 g polyester toy filling

Red colored pencil

Use size U.S. 2/3 (3 mm) knitting needles.

DOLL

BODY AND HEAD
The body and head are knitted together from the bottom of the body up and include the underpants and shirt.

Front
Make 1

❋ Cast on 13 sts in white.

❋ Work 7 rows in st st, beg with a K row.

❋ Next row: K.

❋ Break white yarn and join red yarn.

❋ Work 13 rows in st st, beg with a K row.

❋ Next row: K.

❋ Break red yarn and join flesh yarn.

❋ Next row: K.

❋ Next row: (p2tog) twice, P to last 4 sts, (p2tog) twice. [9 sts]

❋ Next row: K1, inc1 into next 6 sts, K2. [15 sts]

❋ Next row: P.

* Next row: K1, inc1, K to last 3 sts, inc1, K2. [17 sts]
* Next row: P.*
* Rep last 2 rows twice more. [21 sts]
* Work 2 rows in st st, beg with a K row.
* Next row: K2, (k2tog) twice, K9, (ssk) twice, K2. [17 sts]
* Next row: p2tog, P to last 2 sts, p2tog. [15 sts]
* Next row: K2, (k2tog) twice, K3, (ssk) twice, K2. [11 sts]
* Next row: p2tog, P to last 2 sts, p2tog. [9 sts]
* Bind off.

Back
Make 1
* Work as for front to *.
* Break flesh yarn and join medium yellow yarn.
* Next row: K1, inc1, K to last 3 sts, inc1, K2. [19 sts]
* Next row: P.
* Rep last 2 rows once more. [21 sts]
* Work 2 rows in st st, beg with a K row.
* Next row: K2, (k2tog) twice, K9, (ssk) twice, K2. [17 sts]
* Next row: p2tog, P to last 2 sts, p2tog. [15 sts]
* Next row: K2, (k2tog) twice, K3, (ssk) twice, K2. [11 sts]
* Next row: p2tog, P to last 2 sts, p2tog. [9 sts]
* Bind off.

LEGS
The boots and legs are knitted as one piece, starting at the sole of the boot.
Make 2
* Cast on 20 sts in dark brown.
* Work 4 rows in st st, beg with a K row.
* Next row: K5, bind off 10 sts, K5. [10 sts]
* Work 4 rows in st st, beg with a P row.
* Next row: K.
* Break dark brown yarn and join royal blue yarn.
* Work 12 rows in st st, beg with a K row.
* Bind off.

ARMS
The arms are knitted from the shoulder to the hand.
Make 2
* Cast on 7 sts in red.
* Work 19 rows in st st, beg with a K row.
* Next row: K.
* Break red yarn and join flesh yarn.
* Work 2 rows in st st, beg with a K row.
* Next row: K1, k2tog, K1, ssk, K1. [5 sts]
* Next row: p2tog, P1, p2tog. [3 sts]
* Next row: s1, k2tog, psso. [1 st]
* Break yarn and pull it through rem st.

MAKING UP
With the two head and body pieces right sides together, whipstitch around the head. Turn the piece right side out and sew the side seams of the body using mattress stitch, leaving the lower edge open for stuffing. Stuff the doll and close the gap using mattress stitch.

Fold one leg in half lengthwise, right sides together, and whipstitch the top and lower edge of the boots. Turn the leg right side out and sew the back seam using mattress stitch. Repeat for the second leg. Stuff the legs and boots.

Fold one arm in half lengthwise, right sides together, and whipstitch around the hand. Turn the arm right side out and sew the long seams of the shirt using mattress stitch. Repeat for the second arm. The arms do not need stuffing.

Sew the arms and legs in place.

Using medium yellow yarn, work a few rows of chain stitch at the front of the head for the hair.

Work two French knots in black yarn for the eyes. Work two circles of chain stitch around each eye using white yarn. Work two short rows of chain stitch in flesh yarn for the nose.

Divide a short length of deep pink yarn into two thinner strands. Work two straight stitches, one over the top of the other, for the mouth. Add color to the cheeks using a red colored pencil.

SHORTS
The shorts are knitted as one piece.
Make 1
* Cast on 16 sts in emerald green.
* Work 7 rows in st st, beg with a P row.
* Break yarn and leave sts on a spare needle or stitch holder.
* Work a second shorts leg exactly as the first, but don't break yarn.
* Next row: K16 sts from second shorts leg, then knit across 16 sts from first shorts leg. [32 sts]
* Work 8 rows in st st, beg with a P row.
* K 2 rows.
* Bind off loosely.

STRAPS
Make 2
* Cast on 24 sts in emerald green.
* Bind off kwise.

MAKING UP
Using mattress stitch, join the back seam of the shorts so that the lowest part of the seam is level with the crotch. Join the two inside leg seams, again using mattress stitch. Put the shorts on the doll and sew the straps in place, crossing them at the back. Sew the buttons to the front of the straps, as shown in the photograph (see page 42).

CAP

Make 1

❄ Cast on 28 sts in dark brown.

❄ K 2 rows.

❄ Next row: P.

❄ Next row: K1, (m1, K1) to end. [55 sts]

❄ Next row: P.

❄ Next row: K.

❄ Next row: Bind off 23 sts, K9, bind off 23 sts. [9 sts]

❄ Break yarn and rejoin it to rs of 9 sts just worked.

❄ Next row: K1, m1, K to last st, m1, K1. [11 sts]

❄ Next row: P.

❄ Rep last 2 rows 4 times more. [19 sts]

❄ Next row: K1, k2tog, K to last 3 sts, ssk, K1. [17 sts]

❄ Next row: P.

❄ Rep last 2 rows 3 times more. [11 sts]

❄ Next row: K1, k2tog, K to last 3 sts, ssk, K1. [9 sts]

❄ Bind off pwise.

PEAK

Make 1

❄ With rs facing, pick up and K 9 sts across the center of the front of the hat.

❄ Next row: P.

❄ Next row: k2tog, K5, ssk. [7 sts]

❄ Next row: p2tog, P3, p2tog. [5 sts]

❄ Next row: inc1, K to last 2 sts, inc1, K1. [7 sts]

❄ Next row: inc1 pwise, P to last 2 sts, inc1 pwise, P1. [9 sts]

❄ Bind off loosely.

MAKING UP

Join the back seam of the side band of the hat. Whipstitch the top of the hat to the side band, working from the inside. Fold the second part of the peak (which will become the lining) upward, so that the right sides of the peak are together. Whipstitch the sides. Turn the peak right side out and whipstitch the edge of the peak facing in place on the inside.

HOW TO KNIT

Gretel

Gretel is probably the most adorable little girl in the world of fairy tales. Here, she is cutely attired in a charming folk dress in rich royal blue and a pair of contrasting bright red stockings. Her hair is arranged in practical braids and her expression is understandably slightly nervous. She'd like to smile—if only life was a little kinder.

GRETEL
MATERIALS

⅛ oz./3 g (7 yd./6.5 m) white DK yarn

⅛ oz./4 g (10 yd./9 m) royal blue DK yarn

⅛ oz./4 g (10 yd./9 m) flesh DK yarn

1/16 oz./1.5 g (4 yd./3.5 m) medium brown DK yarn

⅛ oz./4 g (10½ yd./9.5 m) red DK yarn

1/16 oz./1 g (2 yd./1.5 m) emerald green DK yarn

1/16 oz./2 g (5½ yd./5 m) dark brown DK yarn

Small amount of black DK yarn

Very small amount of deep pink DK yarn

⅜–½ oz./10–15 g polyester toy filling

Red colored pencil

Use size U.S. 2/3 (3 mm) knitting needles except when instructed to use size U.S. 2 (2.75 mm) knitting needles.

DOLL

BODY AND HEAD

The body and head are knitted together from the bottom of the body upward and include the underpants and bodice of the dress.

Front
Make 1
* Cast on 13 sts in white.
* Work 7 rows in st st, beg with a K row.
* Next row: K.
* Break white yarn and join royal blue yarn.
* Work 11 rows in st st, beg with a K row.
* Next row: K.
* Break royal blue yarn and join flesh yarn.
* Next row: K.
* Next row: (p2tog) twice, P to last 4 sts, (p2tog) twice. [9 sts]
* Next row: K1, inc1 into next 6 sts, K2. [15 sts]
* Next row: P.

* Next row: K1, inc1, K to last 3 sts, inc1, K2. [17 sts]
* Next row: P.*
* Rep last 2 rows twice more. [21 sts]
* Work 2 rows in st st, beg with a K row.
* Next row: K2, (k2tog) twice, K9, (ssk) twice, K2. [17 sts]
* Next row: p2tog, P to last 2 sts, p2tog. [15 sts]
* Next row: K2, (k2tog) twice, K3, (ssk) twice, K2. [11 sts]
* Next row: p2tog, P to last 2 sts, p2tog. [9 sts]
* Bind off.

Back
Make 1
* Work as for front to *.
* Break flesh yarn and join medium brown yarn.
* Next row: K1, inc1, K to last 3 sts, inc1, K2. [19 sts]
* Next row: P.
* Rep last 2 rows once more. [21 sts]
* Work 2 rows in st st, beg with a K row.
* Next row: K2, (k2tog) twice, K9, (ssk) twice, K2. [17 sts]

* Next row: p2tog, P to last 2 sts, p2tog. [15 sts]
* Next row: K2, (k2tog) twice, K3, (ssk) twice, K2. [11 sts]
* Next row: p2tog, P to last 2 sts, p2tog. [9 sts]
* Bind off.

LEGS
The feet and legs are knitted as one piece, starting at the sole of the foot.
Make 2
* Cast on 20 sts in red.
* Work 4 rows in st st, beg with a K row.
* Next row: K5, bind off 10 sts, K5. [10 sts]
* Work 15 rows in st st, beg with a P row.
* Bind off.

ARMS
The arms are knitted from the shoulder to the hand.
Make 2
* Cast on 7 sts in royal blue.
* Work 7 rows in st st, beg with a K row.
* Next row: K.

* Next row: P.
* Break royal blue yarn and join flesh yarn.
* Work 11 rows in st st, beg with a P row.
* Next row: K1, k2tog, K1, ssk, K1. [5 sts]
* Next row: p2tog, P1, p2tog. [3 sts]
* Next row: s1, k2tog, psso. [1 st]
* Break yarn and pull it through rem st.

MAKING UP

With the two head and body pieces right sides together, whipstitch around the head. Turn the piece right side out and sew the side seams of the body using mattress stitch, leaving the lower edge open for stuffing. Stuff the doll and close the gap using mattress stitch.

Fold one leg in half lengthwise, right sides together, and whipstitch the top and lower edge of the foot. Turn the leg right side out and sew the back seams using mattress stitch. Repeat for the second leg. Stuff the legs and feet.

Fold one arm in half lengthwise, right sides together, and whipstitch around the hand. Turn the arm right side out and sew the long seam using mattress stitch. Repeat for the second arm. The arms do not need stuffing.

Sew the arms and legs in place.

Split a length of red yarn into two thinner strands and use one of these to embroider two cross shapes on the front of the bodice, as shown in the photograph (see page 44).

Using light brown yarn, work a few rows of chain stitch at the front of the head for the hair, using the photograph as a guide. For the braids, cut six 14-in. (35-cm) lengths of light brown yarn. Thread three lengths through one corner of the head so that you have six shorter lengths. Divide these shorter lengths into three groups of two strands and braid them. Use two strands to tie around the bottom of the braids to secure them. Make the second braid in the same way.

Work two French knots in black yarn for the eyes. Work two circles of chain stitch around each eye, using white yarn.

Using a single ply of black yarn, work three straight stitches above each eye to represent the eyelashes. Work two short rows of chain stitch in flesh yarn for the nose.

Divide a short length of deep pink yarn into two thinner strands. Work two straight stitches, one over the top of the other, for the mouth. Add color to the cheeks using a red colored pencil.

DRESS SKIRT

Make 1
* Cast on 38 sts in royal blue.
* Work 3 rows in st st, beg with a P row.
* Leave royal blue yarn at side and join emerald green yarn.
* K 2 rows. Break emerald green yarn and use royal blue yarn.
* Work 10 rows in st st, beg with a K row.
* Next row: (k2tog) 9 times, K2, (ssk) 9 times. [20 sts]
* K 2 rows.
* Bind off.

MAKING UP

Sew the back seam of the skirt using mattress stitch. Whipstitch the skirt in place around the waist of the doll.

APRON

Make 1
* Cast on 12 sts in white leaving a tail approx. 12 in. (30 cm) long.
* K 2 rows.
* Next row: K2, P to last 2 sts, K2.
* Next row: K.
* Next row: K2, P to last 2 sts, K2.
* Rep last 2 rows twice more.
* Next row: k2tog, K to last 2 sts, ssk. [10 sts]
* Rep last row once more. [8 sts]
* Bind off pwise, leaving a tail approx. 12 in. (30 cm) long.

MAKING UP

Thread the tail from binding off up the side of the apron and secure it at the top. Using the two tails, work two crochet chains approximately 3 in. (7 cm) long for the apron ties.

SHOES

Make 2
* Using size U.S. 2 (2.75 mm) needles, cast on 8 sts in dark brown.
* 1st row: inc1, K to last 2 sts, inc1, K1. [10 sts]
* Next row: P.
* Rep last 2 rows once more. [12 sts]
* Work 2 rows in st st, beg with a K row.
* Next row: inc1, K to last 2 sts, inc1, K1. [14 sts]
* Next row: P5, bind off 4 sts pwise, P to end. Turn work and cont on only these last 5 sts, leaving rem sts on needle or on a safety pin.
* Work 6 rows in st st, beg with a K row.
* Bind off.
* With rs facing, rejoin yarn to rem 5 sts.
* Work 6 rows in st st, beg with a K row.
* Bind off.

MAKING UP

Fold the shoe pieces in half lengthwise with the right side facing inward. Whipstitch the back and lower seam of the shoes. Turn the right way out. Put the shoes on the doll and secure with a couple of stitches. Work a couple of large straight stitches across the foot to represent the bar of the shoe.

HOW TO KNIT
The Wicked Witch

If there is a more gruesome fairy-tale character than this wicked witch in the tale of Hansel and Gretel, then she must be a very, very bad person. This child-hating old woman, complete with a weird tooth and warts, wears an ancient grubby dress and drab coat—but she's plenty of fun to knit and the perfect antidote to knitting the sweet-natured Hansel and Gretel.

MATERIALS

¼ oz./6 g (15½ yd./14 m) flesh DK yarn

¼ oz./5 g (13 yd./12 m) gray DK yarn

¼ oz./7 g (18½ yd./17 m) light olive green DK yarn

⅛ oz./3 g (8 yd./7 m) dark brown DK yarn

¼ oz./5 g (13 yd./12 m) brown/green DK yarn

¾ oz./20 g (55 yd./50 m) medium blue DK yarn

Small amounts of black and white DK yarns

Very small amounts of pink and camel DK yarns

One medium gray button

One snap fastener

White sewing thread

⅜–½ oz./10–15 g polyester toy filling

Use size U.S. 2/3 (3 mm) knitting needles except when instructed to use size U.S. 5 (3.75 mm) knitting needles.

DOLL

HEAD

The head is knitted from the forehead down to the chin.

Front

Make 1
* Cast on 12 sts in flesh.
* 1st row: inc1, K to last 2 sts, inc1, K1. [14 sts]
* Next row: P.
* Next row: K2, m1, K to last 2 sts, m1, K2. [16 sts]
* Next row: P.*
* Rep last 2 rows once more. [18 sts]
* Work 8 rows in st st, beg with a K row.
* Next row: K2, (k2tog) twice, K to last 6 sts, (ssk) twice, K2. [14 sts]
* Next row: p2tog, P to last 2 sts, p2tog. [12 sts]
* Next row: K2, (k2tog) twice, K to last 6 sts, (ssk) twice, K2. [8 sts]
* Bind off pwise.

Back

Make 1
* Work as for front to *.
* Break flesh yarn and join gray yarn.
* Next row: K2, m1, K to last 2 sts, m1, K2. [18 sts]
* Work 9 rows in st st, beg with a P row.
* Next row: K2, (k2tog) twice, K to last 6 sts, (ssk) twice, K2. [14 sts]
* Next row: p2tog, P to last 2 sts, p2tog. [12 sts]
* Next row: K2, (k2tog) twice, K to last 6 sts, (ssk) twice, K2. [8 sts]
* Bind off pwise.

BODY

The body is knitted from the lower edge to the neck edge. The underpants and top are knitted as part of the body.
Make 2 pieces
* Cast on 22 sts in gray.
* Work 7 rows in st st, beg with a K row.
* Next row: K.
* Break gray yarn and join light olive green yarn.
* Work 10 rows in st st, beg with a K row.

* Next row: K2, k2tog, K to last 4 sts, ssk, K2. [20 sts]
* Next row: P.
* Rep last 2 rows once more. [18 sts]
* Bind off.

LEGS

The boots and legs are knitted as one piece, starting at the sole of the boot.
Make 2
* Cast on 24 sts in dark brown.
* Work 4 rows in st st beg with a K row.
* Next row: K7, bind off 10 sts, K to end. [14 sts]
* Work 4 rows in st st, beg with a P row.
* Next row: K.
* Break dark brown yarn and join flesh yarn.
* Work 12 rows in st st, beg with a K row.
* Bind off loosely.

ARMS

The arms are knitted from the shoulder to the hand.
Make 2
* Cast on 10 sts in light olive green.
* Work 15 rows in st st, beg with a K row.
* Next row: K.
* Break light olive green yarn and join flesh yarn.
* Work 2 rows in st st, beg with a K row.
* Next row: k2tog, K6, ssk. [8 sts]
* Next row: p2tog, P4, p2tog. [6 sts]
* Next row: k2tog, K2, ssk. [4 sts]
* Break yarn, thread it through rem sts, and secure.

HAIR

* Using size U.S. 5 (3.75 mm) needles, cast on 15 sts in gray.
* 1st row: K, but for every stitch wind the yarn around the needle 3 times instead of the usual once (see Extended Garter Stitch, page 11).
* Next row: K each stitch, dropping the extra loops.
* Bind off.

MAKING UP

Place the two head pieces right sides together and whipstitch around the edges, leaving the top of the head open for turning and stuffing. Turn the head right side out, stuff, and close the gap using mattress stitch. Sew the body together using mattress stitch, leaving the lower edge open for turning and stuffing. Stuff and close the gap. Sew the head to the body.

Fold one leg in half lengthwise, right sides together, and whipstitch the top and lower edge of the boot. Turn the leg right side out and sew the back seam using mattress stitch. Repeat for the second leg. Stuff the legs and boots.

Fold one arm in half lengthwise, right sides together, and whipstitch around the hand. Turn the arm right side out and sew the long seam using mattress stitch. Repeat for the second arm. The arms do not need stuffing.

Sew the arms and legs in place.

Fold the hair strip in half lengthwise and whipstitch it to the top of the head.

Work two French knots in black yarn for the eyes—one high up the face and one lower down. Work a circle of chain stitch around one eye and two circles of chain stitch around the other eye using white yarn. Using flesh yarn, work a couple of straight stitches at the top of each eye to represent the eyelids. Using flesh yarn, work a flattened coil of chain stitches for the nose. Using camel yarn, work a few French knots to represent warts.

Divide a short length of pink yarn into two thinner strands. Work two straight stitches, one over the top of the other, for the mouth. Using a strand of white yarn, work a couple of small straight stitches, one on top of the other, for the tooth.

TUNIC

Make 2 pieces
* Using size U.S. 5 (3.75 mm) needles, cast on 16 sts in brown/green.
* 1st row: K.
* Next row: K, but for every stitch wind the yarn around your needle twice instead of the usual once.

* Next row: K each stitch, dropping the extra loops (see Extended Garter Stitch, page 11).
* Rep last 2 rows 5 times more.
* Next row: Maintaining the extended garter stitch technique, k2tog, K to last 2 sts, ssk. [14 sts]
* Next row: K each stitch, dropping the extra loops.
* Rep last 2 rows once more. [12 sts]
* Next row: K, but for every stitch wind the yarn around your needle twice instead of the usual once.
* Next row: K each stitch, dropping the extra loops.
* Rep last 2 rows twice more.
* Bind off loosely.

MAKING UP
Whipstitch the tunic together at the shoulders and side seams, leaving enough room for the arms and head.

COAT
The main part of the coat is knitted as one piece from the neck edge down. The sleeves and hood are sewn on separately.
Make 1
* Cast on 36 sts in medium blue.
* K 2 rows.
* Next row: K2, P8. Turn work and cont on only these 10 sts, leaving rem sts on needle.
* Next row: K.
* Next row: K2, P8.
* Rep last 2 rows twice more.
* Break yarn and join it to rem sts on ws of work.
* Next row: P16. Turn work and cont on only these 16 sts, leaving rem sts on needle.
* Work 6 rows in st st, beg with a K row.
* Break yarn and join it to rem 10 sts on ws of work.
* Next row: P8, K2.
* Next row: K.
* Rep these rows twice more.
* Next row: P8, K2.

* Now work across all 36 sts.
* Next row: K8, m1, K4, m1, K12, m1, K4, m1, K8. [40 sts]
* Next and every ws row unless stated: K2, P to last 2 sts, K2.
* Next rs row: K.
* Next rs row: K9, m1, K4, m1, K14, m1, K4, m1, K9. [44 sts]
* Next rs row: K.
* Next row: K.
* K 3 rows.
* Next row: (K2, m1) to last 2 sts, K2. [65 sts]
* Next row: K2, P to last 2 sts, K2.
* Work 13 rows in st st, beg with a K row and knitting 2 sts at the beg and end of every ws row.
* K 4 rows.
* Bind off.

SLEEVES
Make 2
* Cast on 16 sts in medium blue.
* Work 8 rows in st st, beg with a K row.
* K 2 rows.
* Bind off.

HOOD
The hood is knitted from the face edge to the back.
Make 1
* Cast on 32 sts in medium blue.
* K 2 rows.
* Work 17 rows in st st, beg with a P row.
* Bind off.

MAKING UP
Sew the seams of the sleeves using mattress stitch. Insert them into the armholes of the coat and whipstitch them in place from the inside.

Fold the hood piece in half widthwise and sew the back seam. Whipstitch the hood in place around the neck edge of the coat. The edges of the hood should come ½ in. (1 cm) in from the front edges of the coat.

Sew the button onto the right side of the coat at the waist. Sew the top of the snap fastener under the button and the bottom of it to the corresponding part of the other side of the coat.

Goldilocks and the Three Bears

Goldilocks's mother believed in independence, so the little girl was allowed to explore the countryside around her home as she pleased. One day, she wandered farther than usual and found herself outside a small house she had never seen before. It was spick-and-span and—tempting for a curious little girl—the door was ajar. Goldilocks went straight in, but no one seemed to be there. They clearly weren't far away, because in the kitchen, three chairs were set around a table, and on the table were three bowls of oatmeal. Goldilocks had walked a long way and was feeling in need of a rest. So she sat down on the biggest chair, but it wasn't comfortable. **"Too hard!"** she cried, switching to the medium-size chair, which was covered in cushions. **"Too soft!"** she pouted, and moved to the smallest chair, which she found just perfect for her. Then she realized she was hungry, too.

So she dipped a spoon in the biggest bowl of oatmeal. But it was too hot. On to the medium-size bowl—but no, that one was too cold. So she tried the small bowl and found it tasted delicious. Adding some honey from a jar on the table, and without thinking that the oatmeal belonged to someone else who might be hungry, too, she ate it all up. Now that she'd eaten, Goldilocks felt sleepy. There were three beds in the adjoining bedroom, a large one, a medium-size one, and a small one. As usual, our heroine tried all three—and, as you'd expect, it was the small one that fitted her the best. So she crawled into the bed and fell fast asleep.

But who owned the house? A family of three bears who had learned of a honey tree and gone out for an hour. They returned, tired and hungry, and sat down at the table to eat. **"Who's been sitting in my chair?"** growled Daddy Bear, and **"Who's been sitting in MY chair?"** shrilled Mother Bear, and **"Who's been sitting in my chair?"** squeaked Baby Bear, **"the cushion is all messed up!"** And it was the same story when it came to the oatmeal: **"Who's tried my oatmeal?"** gruffed Daddy Bear. **"And mine!"** said Mother Bear. **"And mine!"** said Baby Bear. **"And they've eaten it all up!"** At that moment, they heard a movement from the bedroom. All three rushed next door. **"Who's been in my bed?"** shouted Daddy Bear. **"And mine!"** called Mother Bear. **"And mine!"** cried Baby Bear, **"And she's still there!"** Goldilocks awoke to find three very angry bears staring down at her. Very much frightened, she jumped out of bed and ran out of the house and all the way home. And these days, she's less inclined to use other people's things without asking first.

Goldilocks

With her tumbling golden hair and demure smile, she looks as pretty as a picture. Dressed so sweetly in pale green and purple, she looks as if she's the kind of girl who would never put a foot out of line. But looks can be deceiving. Goldilocks is a girl who knows just what she wants. And when she went walking in the woods near her home, she started to feel a little peckish. So why not just slip into that charming little house and help herself to some breakfast? No one will care, will they?

MATERIALS

1/16 oz./2 g (4½ yd./4 m) pale pink DK yarn
1/8 oz./3.5 g (9½ yd./8.5 m) pale green DK yarn
¼ oz./6 g (16½ yd./15 m) flesh DK yarn
1/16 oz./2 g (5 yd./4.5 m) deep yellow DK yarn
1/8 oz./3 g (7 yd./6.5 m) white DK yarn
¼ oz./7.5 g (20 yd./18 m) purple DK yarn
1/16 oz./2 g (5½ yd./5 m) red DK yarn
Small amount of black DK yarn
3/8–½ oz. (10–15 g) polyester toy filling
Red colored pencil

Use size U.S. 2/3 (3 mm) knitting needles except when instructed to use size U.S. 2 (2.75 mm) knitting needles.

DOLL

BODY AND HEAD
The body and head are knitted together from the bottom of the body up and include the underpants and top.

Front
Make 1
❋ Cast on 13 sts in pale pink.
❋ Work 7 rows in st st, beg with a K row.
❋ Next row: K.
❋ Break pale pink yarn and join pale green yarn.
❋ Work 13 rows in st st, beg with a K row.
❋ Next row: K.
❋ Break pale green yarn and join flesh yarn.
❋ Next row: K.
❋ Next row: (p2tog) twice, P to last 4 sts, (p2tog) twice. [9 sts]
❋ Next row: K1, inc1 into next 6 sts, K2. [15 sts]
❋ Next row: P.
❋ Next row: K1, inc1, K to last 3 sts, inc1, K2. [17 sts]
❋ Next row: P. *
❋ Rep last 2 rows 3 times more. [23 sts]
❋ Work 2 rows in st st, beg with a K row.
❋ Next row: K2, (k2tog) twice, K11, (ssk) twice, K2. [19 sts]
❋ Next row: p2tog, P to last 2 sts, p2tog. [17 sts]

* Next row: K2, (k2tog) twice, K5, (ssk) twice, K2. [13 sts]
* Next row: p2tog, P to last 2 sts, p2tog. [11 sts]
* Bind off.

Back
Make 1
* Work as for front to *.
* Break flesh yarn and join deep yellow yarn.
* Next row: K1, inc1, K to last 3 sts, inc1, K2. [19 sts]
* Next row: P.
* Rep last 2 rows twice more. [23 sts]
* Work 2 rows in st st, beg with a K row.
* Next row: K2, (k2tog) twice, K11, (ssk) twice, K2. [19 sts]
* Next row: p2tog, P to last 2 sts, p2tog. [17 sts]
* Next row: K2, (k2tog) twice, K5, (ssk) twice, K2. [13 sts]
* Next row: p2tog, P to last 2 sts, p2tog. [11 sts]
* Bind off.

LEGS
The socks and legs are knitted as one piece, starting at the sole of the foot.
Make 2
* Cast on 22 sts in white.
* Work 4 rows in st st, beg with a K row.
* Next row: K5, bind off 12 sts, K5. [10 sts]
* Work 6 rows in st st, beg with a P row.
* Next row: K.
* Break white yarn and join flesh yarn.
* Work 10 rows in st st, beg with a K row.
* Bind off.

ARMS
The arms are knitted from the shoulder to the hand.
Make 2
* Cast on 7 sts in pale green.
* Work 7 rows in st st, beg with a K row.
* Next row: K.
* Break pale green yarn and join flesh yarn.
* Work 12 rows in st st, beg with a K row.
* Next row: K1, k2tog, K1, ssk, K1. [5 sts]
* Next row: p2tog, P1, p2tog. [3 sts]
* Next row: s1, k2tog, psso. [1 st]
* Break yarn and pull it through rem st.

MAKING UP
With the two head and body pieces right sides together, whipstitch around the head. Turn the piece right side out and sew the side seams using whipstitch, leaving the lower edge open for stuffing. Stuff the doll and close the gap using mattress stitch.

Fold the legs in half lengthwise, right sides together, and whipstitch the top and lower edge of the feet. Turn right sides out and sew the back seam, using mattress stitch, and stuff.

Fold the arms in half lengthwise, right sides together, and whipstitch around the hands. Turn right sides out and sew the long seam using mattress stitch. The arms do not need stuffing.

Sew the arms and legs in place.

Using deep yellow yarn, work a few rows of chain stitch at the front of the head for the hair. Make four 4½-in. (12-cm) crochet chains and arrange into loops at each side of the head.

Work two French knots in black yarn for the eyes. Work two circles of chain stitch around each eye using white yarn. Using a separated ply of black yarn, work three straight stitches above each eye for the eyelashes. Work two short rows of chain stitch in flesh yarn for the nose.

Using red yarn, work two straight stitches side by side for the mouth, so that they form a flattened V shape. Add color to the cheeks using a red colored pencil.

DRESS
Make 2 pieces
* Cast on 20 sts in purple.
* 1st row: K.
* Work 3 rows in st st, beg with a K row.
* Next row: K.
* Work 4 rows in st st, beg with a K row.
* Next row: K2, k2tog, K to last 3 sts, ssk, K1. [18 sts]
* Work 3 rows in st st, beg with a P row.
* Rep last 4 rows once more. [16 sts]
* Work 7 rows in st st, beg with a K row.
* K 3 rows.
* Next row: Bind off 2 sts, K2 (3 sts on needle incl st rem from binding off), bind off 6 sts, K to end. [8 sts]

* Work on only 5 sts just knitted, leaving rem 3 sts on needle.
* Next row: Bind off 2 sts, K to end. [3 sts]
* Working on only 3 sts just knitted, K 7 rows.
* Bind off.
* With ws facing, rejoin yarn to 3 sts left on needle.
* K 8 rows.
* Bind off.

MAKING UP
Sew the shoulder and side seams.

SHOES
Make 2
* Using size U.S. 2 (2.75 mm) needles, cast on 8 sts in red.
* 1st row: inc1, K to last 2 sts, inc1, K1. [10 sts]
* Next row: P.
* Rep last 2 rows once more. [12 sts]
* Work 2 rows in st st, beg with a K row.
* Next row: inc1, K to last 2 sts, inc1, K1. [14 sts]
* Next row: P5, bind off 4 sts pwise, P to end. Turn work and cont on only these last 5 sts, leaving rem sts on needle or on a safety pin.
* Work 6 rows in st st, beg with a K row.
* Bind off.
* With rs facing, rejoin yarn to rem 5 sts.
* Work 6 rows in st st, beg with a K row.
* Bind off.

MAKING UP
Fold the shoe pieces in half lengthwise with the right side facing inward. Whipstitch the back and lower seam of the shoes. Turn the right way out. Put the shoes on the doll and secure with a couple of stitches. Work a couple of large straight stitches across the foot to represent the bar of the shoe.

BOW
Make 1
Work an 3-in. (8-cm) crochet chain in purple. Arrange it in a figure-eight shape with the yarn tails at the center, and use these yarn tails to sew the bow to the head.

Father Bear

Father bear is definitely the head of the three bears' household. He has the biggest bed, the biggest chair, and, of course, the biggest bowl of oatmeal. In his red shirt and green pants with suspenders, he's a traditional type of bear. But his stern expression and burly build give you a hint that you would be wise not to get on his bad side.

MATERIALS

½ oz./15 g (40½ yd./37 m) pale mustard DK yarn

¼ oz./8 g (22 yd./20 m) red DK yarn

⅜ oz./11 g (30 yd./27 m) green DK yarn

Small amounts of white and black DK yarns

Two small red buttons

⅜–½ oz. (10–15 g) polyester toy filling

Green sewing thread

Use size U.S. 2/3 (3 mm) knitting needles.

DOLL

BODY

The body is knitted from the bottom edge up and includes the body of the shirt (the shirt sleeves are knitted separately).

Make 2 pieces

❋ Cast on 18 sts in pale mustard.

❋ 1st row: inc1, K to last 2 sts, inc1, K1. [20 sts]

❋ Next row: P.

❋ Next row: K2, m1, K to last 2 sts, m1, K2. [22 sts]

❋ Next row: P.

❋ Rep last 2 rows once more. [24 sts]

❋ Work 8 rows in st st, beg with a K row.

❋ Break pale mustard yarn and join red yarn.

❋ K 2 rows.

❋ Work 6 rows in st st, beg with a K row.

❋ Next row: K2, k2tog, K to last 4 sts, ssk, K2. [22 sts]

❋ Work 3 rows in st st, beg with a P row.

❋ Next row: K2, k2tog, K to last 4 sts, ssk, K2. [20 sts]

❋ Next row: P.

❋ Rep last 2 rows 4 times more. [12 sts]

❋ K 2 rows.

❋ Bind off.

HEAD

The head is knitted from the back
to the nose.
Make 2 pieces
❊ Cast on 14 sts in pale mustard.
❊ 1st row: inc1, K to last 2 sts, inc1, K1.
  [16 sts]
❊ Next row: P.
❊ Next row: K2, m1, K to last 2 sts, m1,
  K2. [18 sts]
❊ Work 11 rows in st st, beg with a P row.
❊ Next row: K2, k2tog, K2, k2tog, K2,
  ssk, K2, ssk, K2. [14 sts]
❊ Next row; P.
❊ Next row: K2, (k2tog) twice, K2, (ssk)
  twice, K2. [10 sts]
❊ Next row: P.
❊ Next row: K.
❊ Next row: p2tog, P6, p2tog. [8 sts]
❊ Next row: k2tog, K4, ssk. [6 sts]
❊ Bind off kwise.

EARS

Make 2
❊ Cast on 5 sts in pale mustard.
❊ Work 2 rows in st st, beg with a K row.
❊ Next row: k2tog, K1, ssk. [3 sts]
❊ Next row: P.
❊ Next row: (K1, m1) twice, K1. [5 sts]
❊ Work 3 rows in st st, beg with a P row.
❊ Bind off.

LEGS

The feet and legs are knitted as one
piece, starting at the sole of the foot.
Make 2
❊ Cast on 26 sts in pale mustard.
❊ Work 5 rows in st st, beg with a K row.
❊ Next row: P4, bind off 18 sts kwise,
  P to end. [8 sts]
❊ Work 8 rows in st st, beg with a K row.
❊ Bind off.

ARMS

The arms are knitted from the shoulder
to the paw.
Make 2
❊ Cast on 8 sts in pale mustard.
❊ Work 16 rows in st st, beg with a K row.
❊ Next row: k2tog, K4, ssk. [6 sts]
❊ Next row: p2tog, P2, p2tog. [4 sts]
❊ Bind off.

MAKING UP

With the two head pieces wrong sides
together, seam the sides using mattress
stitch, leaving the back edge open for
stuffing. Stuff the head and close the gap
using mattress stitch. With the two body
pieces wrong sides together, seam the
sides and lower edge using mattress stitch.
Stuff the body through the neck edge.
Position the head on the neck so that the
neck forms a circle on the underside of
the head and sew it in place.

Fold one leg in half lengthwise, right
sides together, and whipstitch the top and
bottom of the foot. Turn the leg right side
out and sew the back seam using mattress
stitch. Repeat for the second leg. Stuff
and sew in place.

Fold one arm in half lengthwise, right
sides together, and whipstitch around
the paw. Turn the arm right side out and
sew the long seam using mattress stitch.
Repeat for the second arm. Stuff the arms
lightly. Sew the arms in place.

Fold the ear pieces right sides
together and whipstitch around the curved
edges. Turn the ears right side out and
sew in place.

Work two French knots in black yarn
for the eyes. Work two circles of chain
stitch around each eye using white yarn.
Using black yarn, work a small triangle
in satin stitch for the nose and add two
straight stitches for the mouth.

SHIRT SLEEVES

The main body of the shirt is knitted
as part of the bear.
Make 2
❊ Cast on 11 sts in red.
❊ Work 12 rows in st st, beg with a
  K row.
❊ Bind off.

MAKING UP

Sew the side seams of the sleeves using
mattress stitch. Whipstitch the bound-off
edges of the sleeves around the top of the
arm and roll up the lower edges.

PANTS

The pants are knitted from the bottom
edge up and are designed to be a loose
fit on the bear.
Make 2 pieces
❊ Cast on 22 sts in green.
❊ 1st row: inc1, K to last 2 sts, inc1, K1.
  [24 sts]
❊ Next row: P.
❊ Next row: K2, m1, K to last 2 sts, m1,
  K2. [26 sts]
❊ Next row: P.
❊ Rep last 2 rows once more. [28 sts]
❊ Work 12 rows in st st, beg with a K row.
❊ K 2 rows.
❊ Bind off pwise.

PANTS LEGS

Make 2
❊ Cast on 14 sts in green.
❊ K 2 rows.
❊ Work 3 rows in st st, beg with a P row.
❊ Bind off.

SUSPENDERS

Make 2
❊ Cast on 34 sts in green.
❊ 1st row: K.
❊ Bind off kwise.

MAKING UP

Join the side and lower seams of the
pants using mattress stitch, leaving two
gaps along the lower edge that match the
position of the legs. Sew the side seams
of the pants legs using mattress stitch.
Insert them into the holes on the lower
edge of the pants and whipstitch them in
place. Put the pants on the bear and sew
the suspenders in place, crossing them
at the back. Using green thread, sew the
buttons to the front of the suspenders as
shown in the photograph (see page 56).

HOW TO KNIT
Mother Bear

Mother bear is a gentle-natured creature who puts her family at the heart of everything she does. Dressed sensibly in a comfortable skirt and cardigan, she gets along with everyone and doesn't like to make a fuss. One of her favorite occupations is cooking good, wholesome meals for her family—such as the oatmeal in this famous story.

MATERIALS

⅛ oz./3.5 g (9½ yd./8.5 m) cream DK yarn
¼ oz./6 g (16½ yd./15 m) pastel pink DK yarn
⅜ oz./9 g (24 yd./22 m) pale mustard DK yarn
¼ oz./6.5 g (17½ yd./16 m) bright pink DK yarn
¼ oz./8 g (22 yd./20 m) aqua DK yarn
Small amounts of white and black DK yarns
One small pink button
One snap fastener
⅜–½ oz. (10–15 g) polyester toy filling
White sewing thread

Use size U.S. 2/3 (3 mm) knitting needles.

DOLL

BODY
The body is knitted from the bottom edge upward and includes the underpants and the shirt.
Make 2 pieces
❋ Cast on 14 sts in cream.
❋ 1st row: inc1, K to last 2 sts, inc1, K1. [16 sts]
❋ Next row: P.
❋ Next row: K2, m1, K to last 2 sts, m1, K2. [18 sts]
❋ Next row: P.
❋ Rep last 2 rows once more. [20 sts]
❋ Work 6 rows in st st, beg with a K row.
❋ Break cream yarn and join pastel pink yarn.
❋ K 2 rows.
❋ Work 6 rows in st st, beg with a K row.
❋ Next row: K2, k2tog, K to last 4 sts, ssk, K2. [18 sts]
❋ Work 3 rows in st st, beg with a P row.
❋ Next row: K2, k2tog, K to last 4 sts, ssk, K2. [16 sts]
❋ Next row: P.
❋ Rep last 2 rows 3 times more. [10 sts]
❋ K 2 rows.
❋ Bind off.

HEAD
The head is knitted from the back of the head to the nose.
Make 2 pieces

* Cast on 12 sts in pale mustard.
* 1st row: inc1, K to last 2 sts, inc1, K1. [14 sts]
* Next row: P.
* Next row: K2, m1, K to last 2 sts, m1, K2. [16 sts]
* Work 9 rows in st st, beg with a P row.
* Next row: K2, (k2tog) twice, K4, (ssk) twice, K2. [12 sts]
* Next row; P.
* Next row: K1, (k2tog) twice, K2, (ssk) twice, K1. [8 sts]
* Next row: P.
* Next row: K.
* Next row: p2tog, P4, p2tog. [6 sts]
* Bind off.

EARS
Make 2
* Cast on 5 sts in pale mustard.
* Work 2 rows in st st, beg with a K row.
* Next row: k2tog, K1, ssk. [3 sts]
* Next row: P.
* Next row: (K1, m1) twice, K1. [5 sts]
* Work 3 rows in st st, beg with a P row.
* Bind off.

LEGS
The feet and legs are knitted as one piece, starting at the sole of the foot.
Make 2
* Cast on 26 sts in pale mustard.
* Work 5 rows in st st, beg with a K row.
* Next row: P4, bind off 18 sts kwise, P to end. [8 sts]
* Work 8 rows in st st, beg with a K row.
* Bind off.

ARMS
The arms are knitted from the shoulder to the paw.
Make 2
* Cast on 8 sts in pastel pink.
* Work 7 rows in st st, beg with a K row.
* Next row: K.
* Break pastel pink yarn and join pale mustard yarn.
* Work 8 rows in st st, beg with a K row.
* Next row: k2tog, K4, ssk. [6 sts]
* Next row: p2tog, P2, p2tog. [4 sts]
* Bind off.

MAKING UP
Sew mother bear together in the same way as father bear, as described on page 57.

Using a single ply of black yarn, work three small straight stitches above each eye for the eyelashes.

SKIRT
Make 2 pieces
* Cast on 30 sts in bright pink.
* 1st row: (K2, P2) to last 2 sts, K2.
* Next row: (P2, K2) to last 2 sts, P2.
* Rep these 2 rows 6 times more.
* Next row: (k2tog, p2tog) 7 times, k2tog. [15 sts]
* Bind off kwise.

MAKING UP
Join the side seams of the skirt using mattress stitch.

CARDIGAN
The main body of the cardigan is knitted as one piece.
Make 1
* Cast on 34 sts in aqua.
* K 2 rows.
* Work 10 rows in st st, beg with a K row.
* Next row: K9, turn, and work on only these 9 sts, leaving rem sts on needle.
* Next row: P7, K2.
* Next row: K.
* Rep last 2 rows once more.
* Break yarn and rejoin it to rs of rem sts.

* Next row: K16, turn, and work on only these 16 sts, leaving rem sts on needle.
* Work 4 rows in st st, beg with a P row.
* Break yarn and rejoin it to rs of rem 9 sts.
* Next row: K.
* Next row: K2, P7.
* Rep last 2 rows once more.
* Next row: K.
* Now work across all 34 sts on needle.
* Next row: K2, P to last 2 sts, K2.
* K 3 rows.
* Bind off.

SLEEVES
Make 2
* Cast on 14 sts in aqua.
* K 2 rows.
* Work 10 rows in st st, beg with a K row.
* Bind off.

MAKING UP
Sew the seams of the sleeves using mattress stitch. Insert them into the armholes of the cardigan and whipstitch them in place from the inside. Using white thread, sew the button onto the right side of the cardigan. Sew the top of the snap fastener under the button and the bottom of the snap fastener on the corresponding part of the other side of the cardigan.

HOW TO KNIT
Baby Bear

Mother bear wouldn't want to know this, but her little son is spoiled rotten. Although he looks adorable in his cute blue overalls, baby bear is prone to more than the odd tantrum when things don't go his way. He's not prepared to share his toys, his chair, or his food with anyone—even a girl as pretty as little Goldilocks.

DOLL

BODY
The body is knitted from the bottom edge up and includes the shirt.
Make 2 pieces
* Cast on 10 sts in pale mustard.
* 1st row: inc1, K to last 2 sts, inc1, K1. [12 sts]
* Next row: P.
* Next row: K2, m1, K to last 2 sts, m1, K2. [14 sts]
* Next row: P.
* Rep last 2 rows once more. [16 sts]
* Work 4 rows in st st, beg with a K row.
* Break pale mustard yarn and join pale blue yarn.
* K 2 rows.
* Work 4 rows in st st, beg with a K row.
* Next row: K2, k2tog, K to last 4 sts, ssk, K2. [14 sts]
* Work 3 rows in st st, beg with a P row.
* Next row: K2, k2tog, K to last 4 sts, ssk, K2. [12 sts]
* Next row: P.
* Rep last 2 rows once more. [10 sts]
* Work 2 rows in st st, beg with a K row.
* K 2 rows.
* Bind off.

HEAD

The head is knitted from the back to the nose.
Make 2 pieces
❋ Cast on 12 sts in pale mustard.
❋ 1st row: inc1, K to last 2 sts, inc1, K1. [14 sts]
❋ Next row: P.
❋ Next row: K2, m1, K to last 2 sts, m1, K2. [16 sts]
❋ Work 7 rows in st st, beg with a P row.
❋ Next row: K2, (k2tog) twice, K4, (ssk) twice, K2. [12 sts]
❋ Next row; P.
❋ Next row: K1, (k2tog) twice, K2, (ssk) twice, K1. [8 sts]
❋ Next row: P.
❋ Next row: K.
❋ Next row: p2tog, P4, p2tog. [6 sts]
❋ Bind off.

EARS

Make 2
❋ Cast on 5 sts in pale mustard.
❋ Work 2 rows in st st, beg with a K row.
❋ Next row: k2tog, K1, ssk. [3 sts]
❋ Next row: P.
❋ Next row: (K1, m1) twice, K1. [5 sts]
❋ Work 3 rows in st st, beg with a P row.
❋ Bind off.

LEGS

The feet and legs are knitted in one piece, starting at the sole of the foot.
Make 2
❋ Cast on 22 sts in pale mustard.
❋ Work 5 rows in st st, beg with a K row.
❋ Next row: P4, bind off 14 sts kwise, P to end. [8 sts]
❋ Work 6 rows in st st, beg with a K row.
❋ Bind off.

ARMS

The arms are knitted from the shoulder to the paw.
Make 2
❋ Cast on 7 sts in pale blue.

❋ Work 7 rows in st st, beg with a K row.
❋ Next row: K.
❋ Break pale blue yarn and join pale mustard yarn.
❋ Work 8 rows in st st, beg with a K row.
❋ Next row: k2tog, K3, ssk. [5 sts]
❋ Next row: p2tog, P1, p2tog. [3 sts]
❋ Next row: s1, k2tog, psso. [1 st]
❋ Break yarn and pull it through rem st.

MAKING UP

Sew baby bear together in the same way as father bear, as described on page 57.

OVERALLS

Front

Make 1
❋ Cast on 14 sts in air force blue.
❋ 1st row: inc1, K to last 2 sts, inc1, K1. [16 sts]
❋ Next row: P.
❋ Next row: K2, m1, K to last 2 sts, m1, K2. [18 sts]
❋ Next row: P.
❋ Rep last 2 rows once more. [20 sts]

❋ Work 8 rows in st st, beg with a K row.
❋ Next row: P. *
❋ Next row: Bind off 6 sts, K7 (8 sts on needle incl st rem from binding off), bind off 6 sts. [8 sts]
❋ Break yarn and rejoin it to rs of work.
❋ Next row: K.
❋ Next row: K1, P to last st, K1.
❋ Rep these 2 rows once more.
❋ K 3 rows.
❋ Bind off pwise.

Back

Make 1
❋ Work as for front until *.
❋ Bind off kwise.

STRAPS

Make 2
❋ Cast on 20 sts in air force blue.
❋ Bind off.

MAKING UP

Join the side and lower seams of the overalls using mattress stitch, leaving two gaps along the lower edge that match the position of the legs. Put the overalls on the bear and sew the straps in place, crossing them at the back.

The Three Little Pigs

It happens at some time to every parent. Poor Mother Pig loved her cute triplets, but she just couldn't afford to keep them any longer. The sty wasn't big enough, their appetites had rocketed—and the noise was getting her down. Luckily, all three piglets shared the same upbeat, can-do attitude. Why, they thought, if there wasn't enough room with their mother, they'd simply build a house of their own, put it together with their own little hands. Better yet, they'd go for one house EACH! Building couldn't be too hard, could it? No sirree!

Piggy No. 1 started first. He drew up a plan and showed it proudly to his brothers: **"Look guys! I'm planning to build my house from straw bales!"** he cried, **"They're light, they're warm, and when I get sick of the view, I can simply tie my home to an oversized balloon and float it to somewhere I prefer!"** He was very, very pleased with his plans. Piggy No. 2 was a little more cautious. **"I think I'll go for sticks to build my house,"** he said. **"I know straw's warm, but it's really light—I'm not sure it's tough enough for a house."** Piggy No. 3 had already decided on his building materials. **"I'm using bricks,"** he said firmly. **"I think traditional is sometimes best."** Off they went, all three, to build their houses.

Not far away, there was a forest. And in the forest there lived a Wolf. The Wolf just loved fresh pork, so when he heard there were three little pigs new to the neighborhood, he came to call. First, he came to the house of straw. It was certainly handsome, gleaming golden in the sun. The Wolf knocked at the door. **"Little pig, little pig, let me come in!"** Piggy No. 1 was horrified. **"Oh no, not by the hairs of my chinny, chin, chin!"** he squealed. **"Then,"** said the Wolf, **"I'll huff, and I'll puff, and I'll blow your house down!"** **"Try it!"** said Piggy No. 1 (he was very scared, but he had spirit). So the Wolf huffed and puffed, and the house blew apart. It was only made of straw, after all. And the Wolf had fresh pork for dinner.

Next day, he went to call on Piggy No. 2. Rapping sharply on the door, he called, **"Little pig, little pig, let me come in!"** Piggy No. 2 had his answer ready: **"Oh no, not by the hairs of my chinny, chin, chin!"** **"Then,"** said the Wolf calmly, **"I'll huff, and I'll puff, and I'll blow your house down!"** The house of wood and twigs was a little stronger than the house of straw, but the Wolf was patient and he blew hard. Eventually, the twig house started to creak and groan—and then suddenly, it blew into little fragments of wood. And the Wolf had pork for dinner again.

His idea had been very successful, so it's hardly surprising that on the third day, the Wolf turned up at the door of the house made of bricks. He lifted the door knocker and let it fall with a thump. **"Little pig, little pig, let me come in!"**

Piggy No. 3 was quick with his answer: **"Oh no, not by the hairs of my chinny, chin, chin!"** "Well, I'll HUFF and I'll PUFF, and I'll BLOW YOUR HOUSE DOWN!" But the Piggy No. 3 just laughed. The Wolf was furious. Filling his lungs, he blew an enormous blow. And the house stayed solid. He drew a deeper breath and tried again. No result. Finally, he breathed in deeper than he'd ever breathed before and blew out a great wind of breath. The house stood still. But the Wolf had gone too far: he'd blown so hard that he'd blown himself inside out and he couldn't turn himself back. So that was the end of him.

And what became of Piggy No. 3? Today, he runs a building business and takes good care of his widowed mother. He always was the brightest of her children.

The Three Little Pigs

Everyone loves a cute piglet, so how much better is it to have three of them? Squishy, pink, and vulnerable, this lovable trio are about to take their first steps into the big, wide world. Their flesh is knitted in the palest of pinks and they are all sporting bright, colorful tops and denim-look shorts.

MATERIALS

FOR EACH PIG
¼ oz./6.5 g (17½ yd./16 m) pale pink DK yarn
1/16 oz./2.5 g (6½ yd./6 m) denim blue DK yarn
Very small amounts of white, black, and mauve
DK yarns
3/8–½ oz. (10–15 g) polyester toy filling

FOR PIG WITH RED SWEATER
1/16 oz./2 g (5½ yd./5 m) red DK yarn
1/16 oz./1.5 g (3½ yd./3 m) cream DK yarn

FOR PIG WITH TURQUOISE SWEATER
⅛ oz./3 g (7 yd./6.5 m) turquoise DK yarn
1/16 oz./1 g (2 yd./1.5 m) cream DK yarn

FOR PIG WITH OLIVE GREEN SWEATER
⅛ oz./3 g (7 yd./6.5 m) olive green
DK yarn
1/16 oz./1 g (2 yd./1.5 m) cream DK yarn

Use size U.S. 2/3 (3 mm) knitting needles
except when instructed to use size U.S. 2
(2.75 mm) knitting needles.

DOLL

BODY AND HEAD
The body and head are knitted together from the bottom of the body up and include the shorts and sweater.
Make 2 pieces
❋ Cast on 12 sts in denim blue.
❋ Work 8 rows in st st, beg with a K row.

For pig with red sweater
❋ Break yarn and join red yarn.
❋ K 2 rows.
❋ Next row: K2, m1, K1, m1, K to last 3 sts, m1, K1, m1, K2. [16 sts]
❋ Next row: P.

❋ Leave red yarn at side of work and join cream yarn.
❋ Work 2 rows in st st, beg with a K row.
❋ Leave cream yarn at side of work and join red yarn.
❋ Work 2 rows in st st, beg with a K row.
❋ Rep last 4 rows once more.
❋ Break cream yarn.
❋ Next row: K2, (k2tog) 3 times, (ssk) 3 times, K2. [10 sts]
❋ Next row: K.
❋ Next row: P.
❋ Break red yarn and join pale pink yarn.
❋ * Next row: P.
❋ Next row: K2, (m1, K1) 3 times, (K1, m1) 3 times, K2. [16 sts]

❋ Next row: P.
❋ Next row: K2, m1, K1, m1, K to last 3 sts, m1, K1, m1, K2. [20 sts]
❋ Work 7 rows in st st, beg with a P row.
❋ Next row: K2, (k2tog) twice, K to last 6 sts, (ssk) twice, K2. [16 sts]
❋ Next row: p2tog, P to last 2 sts, p2tog. [14 sts]
❋ Next row: (k2tog) twice, K to last 4 sts, (ssk) twice. [10 sts]
❋ Bind off kwise.

For pig with turquoise sweater
❋ Break yarn and join turquoise yarn.
❋ K 2 rows.

* Next row: K2, m1, K1, m1, K to last
  3 sts, m1, K1, m1, K2. [16 sts]
* Work 3 rows in st st, beg with a P row.
* Leave turquoise yarn at side of work
  and join cream yarn.
* Work 2 rows in st st, beg with a K row.
* Break cream yarn and rejoin
  turquoise yarn.
* Work 4 rows in st st, beg with a K row.
* Next row: K2, (k2tog) 3 times, (ssk)
  3 times, K2. [10 sts]
* Next row: K.
* Next row: P.
* Break turquoise yarn and join pale
  pink yarn.
* Continue as for pig with red sweater
  from *.

For pig with olive green sweater

* Break yarn and join olive green yarn.
* K 2 rows.
* Leave olive green yarn at side of work
  and join cream yarn.
* Next row: K2, m1, K1, m1, K to last
  3 sts, m1, K1, m1, K2. [16 sts]
* Next row: P.
* Break cream yarn and rejoin olive
  green yarn.
* Work 8 rows in st st, beg with a K row.
* Next row: K2, (k2tog) 3 times,
  (ssk) 3 times, K2. [10 sts]
* Next row: K.
* Next row: P.
* Break olive green yarn and join pale
  pink yarn.
* Continue as for pig with red sweater
  from *.

LEGS

The legs are knitted from the top edge
downward.
Make 2
* Cast on 10 sts in denim blue.
* Work 5 rows in st st, beg with a K row.
* Next row: K.
* Break yarn and join pale pink yarn.
* Next row: k2tog, K to last 2 sts, ssk.
  [8 sts]
* Work 11 rows in st st, beg with a P row.
* Next row: (k2tog) twice, (ssk) twice. [4 sts]
* Break yarn and thread it through rem
  sts. Pull up tightly and secure.

ARMS

The arms are knitted from the top edge
downward.
Make 2

For pig with red sweater

* Cast on 8 sts in red.
* Work 2 rows in st st, beg with a K row.
* Leave red yarn at side of work and join
  cream yarn.
* Work 2 rows in st st, beg with a K row.
* Leave cream yarn at side of work and
  join red yarn.
* Work 2 rows in st st, beg with a K row.
* Leave red yarn at side of work and join
  cream yarn.
* Work 2 rows in st st, beg with a K row.
  Break cream yarn.
* K 2 rows in red yarn. Break red yarn
  and join pale pink yarn.
* Work 4 rows in st st, beg with a K row.
* Next row: (k2tog) twice, (ssk) twice.
  [4 sts]
* Thread yarn through rem sts. Pull up
  tightly and secure.

For pig with turquoise sweater

* Cast on 8 sts in turquoise.
* Work 8 rows in st st, beg with a K row.
* K 2 rows.
* Break turquoise yarn and join pale
  pink yarn.
* Work 4 rows in st st, beg with a K row.
* Next row: (k2tog) twice, (ssk) twice.
  [4 sts]
* Thread yarn through rem sts. Pull up
  tightly and secure.

For pig with olive green sweater

* Cast on 8 sts in olive green.
* Work 8 rows in st st, beg with a K row.
* K 2 rows.
* Break olive green yarn and join pale
  pink yarn.
* Work 4 rows in st st, beg with a K row.
* Next row: (k2tog) twice, (ssk) twice.
  [4 sts]
* Thread yarn through rem sts. Pull up
  tightly and secure.

EARS

Make 2
* Using size U.S. 2 (2.75 mm) needles,
  cast on 4 sts in pale pink.
* 1st row: inc1, K1, inc1, K1. [6 sts]
* K 3 rows.
* Next row: k2tog, K2, ssk. [4 sts]
* Next row: K.
* Next row: k2tog, ssk. [2 sts]
* Next row: K.
* Next row: k2tog. Break yarn and pull it
  through rem st.

SNOUT

Make 1
* Using size U.S. 2 (2.75 mm) needles,
  cast on 4 sts in pale pink.
* 1st row: inc1, K1, inc1, K1. [6 sts]
* Next row: P.
* Next row: k2tog, K2, ssk. [4 sts]
* Bind off kwise.

MAKING UP

With the two head and body pieces
right sides together, whipstitch around the
head. Turn the piece right side out and
sew the side seams in matching yarns
using mattress stitch, leaving the lower
edge open for stuffing. Stuff the pig and
sew the gap closed.

Fold the arm and leg pieces right
sides together and whipstitch around the
hands and feet. Turn the pieces the right
side out and sew the long seams using
mattress stitch.

Stuff the arms and legs and sew
in place.

Sew the ears in place, curving the
lower edge slightly.

Whipstitch the snout in place.

Work two French knots for
the eyes using black yarn.
Work two circles of chain
stitch around each eye
using white yarn.

On the snout, work
two French knots for the
nostrils using mauve yarn.

Work a straight
stitch for the mouth
using a separated ply
of black yarn.

Beauty and the Beast

Beauty was rightly named. She was pretty and she was kind. And her sisters (she had two) were so ugly, greedy, and mean that she looked even better next to them. She was her father's favorite, too. When the merchant asked his girls what he should bring them from a trip into town, the older two demanded fine dresses and jewels. Little Beauty only wanted a red rose. Halfway home, Beauty's father realized that he'd forgotten her simple gift, but he was passing a grand house with a whole hedge of roses, so he picked one for her. Immediately, there was a great roar and a hideous Beast rushed up and called him a thief. Trembling, the merchant explained that he wanted the rose for his youngest daughter. And the Beast gave him a horrible choice: He could be killed at once, or he could fetch Beauty back to live with the Beast and keep him company.

The merchant was sad and didn't know what to do. He returned home, but decided he should go back and die instead of sending Beauty into the Beast's clutches. He said good-bye to his daughters. The elder two were too busy trying on their new finery to pay much attention. However, Beauty listened to the story and talked her father into letting her go in his stead. **"I expect the Beast is just lonely,"** she said gently. **"Perhaps I can change his ways."** Yet even Beauty trembled when she first set eyes on the Beast's horrible features. She told herself firmly that looks were not important, and kept busy by cooking him nutritious meals and tidying up the huge, gloomy house. Over the months that followed, she even became somewhat fond of him.

On one thing she stood firm: Every week he asked her to marry him, and every week she refused and had to sit calmly while he ranted and raved about her ingratitude. A whole year passed and Beauty was desperate to visit her family. Very reluctantly, the Beast gave her permission, but he made her promise she'd stay away only a month. She agreed, but when she reached home she was so delighted to see her friends again that she forgot her promise. The month ended, another passed, and she still hadn't thought about going back.

One day, Beauty was arranging her hair and when she looked in the mirror, instead of her own lovely face, she saw instead a reflection of the Beast, lying ill in his rose garden. Beauty was horrified. Pausing only to say good-bye to her father, she went back to the mansion right away. She found the Beast in the yard, barely conscious and terribly thin. Crying at the sight of him, she helped him up, hugging and kissing him tenderly. **"I've been selfish and thoughtless,"** she sobbed. **"Dear Beast, if you still want me to, I'll marry you!"** And as the words left her lips, something happened: All of a sudden, the Beast transformed into a young man, tall, handsome, and smiling.

He explained to the astounded Beauty that he had been placed under a spell by a wicked fairy, who had decreed that he would remain a Beast until a lovely girl agreed to have him as a husband. So Beauty married the prince and everyone was thrilled for them. Except the ugly sisters, of course—they were positively eaten up with jealousy.

HOW TO KNIT

Beauty

Beautiful, kind, spirited, and intelligent—Beauty was almost perfect. But like any girl, she had dreams of marrying a handsome prince. An ugly monster was not going to make the grade, even if he did happen to be rich and good-hearted. She is clothed here in a classic-style dress in shades of deep gold and pale yellow that beautifully complement her long, dark brown tresses.

MATERIALS

¼ oz./6 g (15½ yd./14 m) beige DK yarn
⅟₁₆ oz./2 g (5½ yd./5 m) dark brown DK yarn
¼ oz./5 g (13 yd./11.5 m) pale yellow DK yarn
¼ oz./8 g (21 yd./19 m) deep yellow DK yarn
⅟₁₆ oz./2 g (5½ yd./5 m) dark pink DK yarn
Small amounts of black and white DK yarns
A very small amount of dark red DK yarn
One medium dark pink flower-shaped button
Two tiny store-bought bows in pale yellow
Two ⅛-in./4-mm gold beads
Gold sewing thread
⅜—½ oz. (10—15 g) polyester toy filling
Pink colored pencil

Use size U.S. 2/3 (3 mm) knitting needles except when instructed to use size U.S. 2 (2.75 mm) knitting needles, and a size D-3 (3.25 mm) crochet hook.

DOLL

HEAD
The head is knitted from the bottom of the chin to the top of the forehead.

Front
Make 1
❋ Cast on 6 sts in beige.
❋ 1st row: K1, inc1, K2, inc1, K1. [8 sts]
❋ Next row: P.
❋ Next row: K1, m1, K to last st, m1, K1. [10 sts]
❋ Next row: P.
❋ Rep last 2 rows twice more.* [14 sts]
❋ Work 10 rows in st st, beg with a K row.
❋ Next row: K2, k2tog, K6, ssk, K2. [12 sts]
❋ Next row: p2tog, P8, p2tog. [10 sts]
❋ Bind off.

Back
Make 1
❋ Work as for front to *.
❋ Break beige yarn and join dark brown yarn.

* Work 10 rows in st st, beg with
  a K row.
* Next row: K2, k2tog, K6, ssk, K2.
  [12 sts]
* Next row: p2tog, P8, p2tog. [10 sts]
* Bind off.

BODY
The body is knitted from the lower edge
to the neck edge.
Make 2 pieces
* Cast on 14 sts in pale yellow.
* Work 6 rows in st st, beg with a K row.
* Next row: K2, (k2tog) twice, K2, (ssk)
  twice, K2. [10 sts]
* Next row: P.
* Next row: K2, k2tog, K2, ssk, K2.
  [8 sts]
* Next row: P.
* Next row: K2, m1, K to last 2 sts, m1,
  K2. [10 sts]
* Next row: P.
* Rep last 2 rows once more. [12 sts]
* Work 3 rows in st st, beg with a K row.
* Next row: K.
* Break pale yellow yarn and join
  beige yarn.
* Work 2 rows in st st, beg with a K row.
* Next row; Bind off 1 st, K to end.
  [11 sts]
* Next row: Bind off 1 st pwise,
  P to end. [10 sts]
* Bind off.

LEGS
The feet and legs are knitted as one
piece, starting at the sole of the foot.
Make 2
* Cast on 24 sts in white.
* Work 4 rows in st st, beg with a K row.
* Next row: K5, bind off 14 sts, K5.
  [10 sts]
* Work 21 rows in st st, beg with a P row.
* Bind off.

ARMS
The arms are knitted from the top of the
shoulder to the tip of the hand.
Make 2
* Cast on 9 sts in beige.
* Work 22 rows in st st, beg with
  a K row.

* Next row: K2, k2tog, K1, ssk, K2. [7 sts]
* Next row: p2tog, P3, p2tog. [5 sts]
* Next row: k2tog, K1, ssk. [3 sts]
* Break yarn and thread through rem sts.

HAIR
* Work six 5¼-in. (13-cm) crochet chains
  in dark brown yarn.

MAKING UP
Place the two head pieces right sides
together and whipstitch around the edges,
leaving the top of the head open for
turning and stuffing. Turn the head right
side out, stuff and close the gap using
mattress stitch. Sew the body together
using mattress stitch, leaving the lower edge
open for turning and stuffing. Stuff and
close the gap. Sew the head to the body.

Fold one leg in half lengthwise, right
sides together, and whipstitch the top and
lower edge of the foot. Turn the leg right
side out and sew the back seam using
mattress stitch. Repeat for the second leg.
Stuff the legs and feet.

Fold one arm in half lengthwise, right
sides together, and whipstitch around
the hand. Turn the arm right side out and
sew the long seam using mattress stitch.
Repeat for the second arm. The arms do
not need stuffing.

Sew the arms and legs in place.

Form each crochet chain into a loop
and join three loops to each side of the
head using the yarn tails.

Work two French knots in black yarn
for the eyes. Work two circles of chain
stitch around each eye using white yarn.
Using a separated ply of black yarn,
work four straight stitches above each
eye to represent the eyelashes. Work two
short rows of chain stitch in flesh yarn for
the nose.

Divide a short length of dark red yarn
into two thinner strands. Work two straight
stitches to form a V shape for the mouth,
then work another set or two of stitches
over these stitches to make the mouth a
little fuller.

Using gold thread, sew the two beads
in position for the earrings. Add color to
the cheeks using a pink colored pencil.

SKIRT OF DRESS

Back
Make 1
* Cast on 24 sts in deep yellow.
* K 2 rows.
* Work 3 rows in st st, beg with a P row.
* Leave deep yellow yarn at the side and
  join pale yellow yarn.
* Work 2 rows in st st, beg with a K row.
* Break pale yellow yarn and use deep
  yellow yarn.
* Work 2 rows in st st, beg with
  a K row.*
* Next row: K2, k2tog, K to last 4 sts,
  ssk, K2. [22 sts]
* Work 3 rows in st st, beg with a P row.
* Rep last 4 rows 3 times more. [16 sts]
* Next row: K2, k2tog, K to last 4 sts,
  ssk, K2. [14 sts]
* Next row: P.
* Bind off pwise.

Front
Make 1
* Work as for back to *.
* Next row: K2, k2tog, K to last 4 sts,
  ssk, K2. [22 sts]
* Work 3 rows in st st, beg with a P row.
* Rep last 4 rows twice more. [18 sts]
* Next row: K2, k2tog, K5. Turn and
  work on only these 8 sts.
* Next row: p2tog, P6. [7 sts]
* Next row: K5, ssk. [6 sts]
* Next row: p2tog, P4. [5 sts]
* Next row: K1, k2tog, ssk. [3 sts]
* Next row: p2tog, P1. [2 sts]
* Next row: k2tog. Break yarn and pull it
  through rem st.
* With rs facing, rejoin yarn to rem 9 sts.
* Next row: K5, ssk, K2. [8 sts]
* Next row: P6, p2tog. [7 sts]
* Next row: k2tog, K5. [6 sts]
* Next row: P4, p2tog. [5 sts]
* Next row: k2tog, ssk, K1. [3 sts]
* Next row: P1, p2tog. [2 sts]
* Next row: k2tog. Break yarn and pull it
  through rem st.

COLLAR

Make 1

❊ Cast on 32 sts in deep yellow.
❊ Work 3 rows in st st, beg with a K row.
❊ Bind off kwise.

MAKING UP

Join the side seams of the skirt using mattress stitch. Whipstitch the back waist of the skirt around the doll's waist and whipstitch the V shape in place at the front. Using deep yellow yarn, work a row of chain stitch at the front of the dress, where the skirt meets the body. Position the collar so that the row edges are at the front and the bound-off edge is at the top. Sew in place at the front and back. Using gold thread, sew the dark pink button in position.

SHOES

Make 2

❊ Using size U.S. 2 (2.75 mm) needles, cast on 8 sts in dark pink.
❊ 1st row: inc1, K to last 2 sts, inc1, K1. [10 sts]
❊ Next row: P.
❊ Rep last 2 rows once more. [12 sts]
❊ Work 2 rows in st st, beg with a K row.
❊ Next row: inc1, K to last 2 sts, inc1, K1. [14 sts]
❊ Next row: P5, bind off 4 sts pwise, P to end. Turn work and cont on only these last 5 sts, leaving rem sts on needle or on a safety pin.
❊ Work 6 rows in st st, beg with a K row.
❊ Bind off.
❊ With rs facing, rejoin yarn to rem sts.
❊ Work 6 rows in st st, beg with a K row.
❊ Bind off.

MAKING UP

Fold the shoe pieces in half lengthwise with the right side facing inward. Whipstitch the back and lower seam of the shoes. Turn the right way out. Put the shoes on the doll and secure with a couple of stitches. Using gold sewing thread, sew the two small bows to the front of the shoes.

HOW TO KNIT
The Beast

Everyone knows that real beauty is on the inside and that it shouldn't matter what a person looks like—but sometimes there are limits. The Beast is an ugly brute, but inside him there is a lovely person struggling to get out! Dressed in casually elegant royal blue and navy, with just a touch of gold to demonstrate his fine status, the Beast does his best to detract from his lack of good looks.

MATERIALS

FOR THE PRINCE

¼ oz./6.5 g (17½ yd./16 m) flesh DK yarn

1/16 oz./1.5 g (3½ yd./3 m) rust DK yarn

¼ oz./5 g (13 yd./12 m) white DK yarn

⅛ oz./4 g (10½ yd./9.5 m) dark olive DK yarn

⅜ oz./9 g (24 yd./22 m) royal blue DK yarn

¼ oz./8 g (21 yd./19 m) navy blue DK yarn

Very small amounts of black and medium pink
DK yarns

Four 5-mm round gold sequins

Four 3-mm gold beads

Two 7-mm square gold sequins

Gold sewing thread

⅜–½ oz. (10–15 g) polyester toy filling

Red colored pencil

FOR THE BEAST MASK AND PAWS

⅛ oz./4.5 g (12 yd./11 m) camel DK yarn

Small amounts of pale green, ocher,
and white DK yarns

Small amount of chunky soft beige yarn

Very small amounts of red and black DK yarns

Use size U.S. 2/3 (3 mm) knitting
needles except when instructed to use
size U.S. 2 (2.75 mm) knitting needles.

DOLL

HEAD

Front
Make 1
❋ Cast on 12 sts in flesh.
❋ 1st row: K1, inc1, K to last 3 sts, inc1,
  K2.* [14 sts]
❋ Work 15 rows in st st, beg with
  a P row.
❋ Next row: K2, k2tog, K to last 4 sts,
  ssk, K2. [12 sts]
❋ Next row: p2tog, P to last 2 sts, p2tog.
  [10 sts]
❋ Rep last 2 rows once more. [6 sts]
❋ Bind off.

Back
Make 1
❋ Work as for front to *.
❋ Work 11 rows in st st, beg with
  a P row.
❋ Break yarn and join rust yarn.
❋ Work 4 rows in st st, beg with a K row.
❋ Next row: K2, k2tog, K to last 4 sts,
  ssk, K2. [12 sts]
❋ Next row: p2tog, P to last 2 sts, p2tog.
  [10 sts]
❋ Rep last 2 rows once more. [6 sts]
❋ Bind off.

EARS
Make 2
❋ Using size U.S. 2 (2.75 mm) needles,
  cast on 4 sts in flesh.
❋ 1st row: (k2tog) twice. [2 sts]
❋ Next row: p2tog.
❋ Break yarn and pull it through rem st.

BODY
Make 2 pieces
❋ Cast on 14 sts in white.
❋ Work 20 rows in st st, beg with
  a K row.
❋ Next row: Bind off 1 st, K to end.
  [13 sts]
❋ Next row: Bind off 1 st pwise,
  P to end. [12 sts]
❋ Bind off.

LEGS

The boots and legs are knitted as one piece, starting at the sole of the boot.
Make 2

✳ Cast on 28 sts in dark olive.
✳ Work 4 rows in st st, beg with a K row.
✳ Next row: K6, bind off 16 sts, K to end. [12 sts]
✳ Work 10 rows in st st, beg with a P row.
✳ Next row: K.
✳ Break dark olive yarn and join flesh yarn.
✳ Work 14 rows in st st, beg with a K row.
✳ Bind off.

ARMS

The arms are knitted from the top of the shoulder to the tip of the hand.
Make 2

✳ Cast on 10 sts in royal blue.
✳ Work 18 rows in st st, beg with a K row.
✳ Break royal blue yarn and join white yarn.
✳ K 4 rows.
✳ Break white yarn and join flesh yarn.
✳ Work 2 rows in st st, beg with a K row.
✳ Next row: K2, k2tog, K2, ssk, K2. [8 sts]
✳ Next row: p2tog, P4, p2tog. [6 sts]
✳ Bind off.

MAKING UP

Place the two head pieces right sides together and whipstitch around the edges, leaving the top of the head open for turning and stuffing. Turn the head right side out, stuff, and close the gap using mattress stitch. Sew the ears in place. Sew the body together using mattress stitch, leaving the lower edge open for turning and stuffing. Stuff and close the gap. Sew the head to the body.

Fold one leg in half lengthwise, right sides together, and whipstitch the top and lower edge of the boot. Turn the leg right side out and sew the back seam using mattress stitch. Repeat for the second leg. Stuff the legs and boots.

Fold one arm in half lengthwise, right sides together, and whipstitch around the hand. Turn the arm right side out and sew the long seam using mattress stitch. Repeat for the second arm. The arms do not need stuffing.

Sew the arms and legs in place. Using gold thread, sew a square sequin to the top of each boot.

Using rust yarn, work a few rows of chain stitch at the front of the head for the hair as shown in the photograph (see page 75).

Work two French knots in black yarn for the eyes. Work two circles of chain stitch around each eye using white yarn. Work two short rows of chain stitch in flesh yarn for the nose.

Using medium pink yarn, work two straight stitches side by side for the mouth, so that they form a flattened V shape. Add color to the cheeks using a red colored pencil.

JACKET FRONTS AND BACK

The two front sides and the back of the jacket are knitted as one piece, from the lower edge to the neck edge. The sleeves have been knitted as part of the doll.
Make 1

✳ Cast on 10 sts in royal blue.
✳ 1st row: K1, inc1, K6, inc1, K1. [12 sts]
✳ Next row: K1, P to last st, K1.
✳ Next row: K1, m1, K to last st, m1, K1. [14 sts]
✳ Next row: K1, P to last st, K1.
✳ Rep last 2 rows twice times more. [18 sts]
✳ Next row: K.
✳ Next row: K1, P to last st, K1
✳ Rep last 2 rows 4 times more.
✳ Next row: Cast on 9 sts, K to end. [27 sts]
✳ Next row: Cast on 9 sts, K9, P18, K to end. [36 sts]
✳ Next row: K.
✳ Next row: K2, P to last 2 sts, K2.
✳ Rep last 2 rows 4 times more.
✳ Next row: K11, turn, and work on only these sts, leaving rem sts on needle.
✳ Next row: P9, K2.
✳ Next row: K.
✳ Next row: P9, K2.
✳ Rep last 2 rows once more.
✳ Next row: K.
✳ Break yarn and leave sts on needle.
✳ With rs facing, join yarn to rem sts.
✳ Next row: K14.
✳ Turn and work on only these sts.
✳ Work 6 rows in st st, beg with a P row.
✳ Break yarn and leave sts on needle.
✳ With rs facing, join yarn to rem 11 sts on left-hand needle.
✳ Next row: K.
✳ Next row: K2, P9.
✳ Next row: K.
✳ Rep last 2 rows twice more.
✳ Now work across all 36 sts on needle.
✳ Next row: Bind off 5 sts kwise, P7 [8 sts on needle, including rem st from binding off], (p2tog) twice, P2, (p2tog) twice, P to end. [27 sts]
✳ Next row: Bind off 5 sts, K to end. [22 sts]
✳ K 2 rows.
✳ Bind off.

MAKING UP

Put the jacket on the doll and whipstitch the armhole edges around the top of the arms. Overlap the jacket fronts and sew the four sequins and beads in place for the buttons.

PANTS

The pants are knitted as one piece.
Make 1

✳ Cast on 14 sts for first leg in navy.
✳ K 2 rows.
✳ Work 23 rows in st st, beg with a P row.
✳ Break yarn and leave sts on spare needle.
✳ Work a second trouser leg exactly as the first, but don't break yarn.

* Next row: K14 sts from second pants leg, then knit across 14 sts from first pants leg. [28 sts]
* Work 9 rows in st st, beg with a P row.
* Next row: (K1, P1) to end.
* Rep last row once more.
* Bind off quite, maintaining the K1, P1 pattern.

MAKING UP

Using mattress stitch, join the back seam so that the lowest part of the seam is level with the crotch. Then join the two inside leg seams, again using mattress stitch.

MASK

Make 2 pieces
* Cast on 22 sts in camel.
* K 2 rows.
* Next row: P.
* Next row: K2, k2tog, K to last 4 sts, ssk, K2. [20 sts]
* Next row: P.
* Rep last 2 rows twice more. [16 sts]
* Work 14 rows in st st, beg with a K row.
* Next row: K2, k2tog, K1, k2tog, K2, ssk, K1, ssk, K2. [12 sts]
* Next row: P.
* Next row: K2, (k2tog) twice, (ssk) twice, K2. [8 sts]
* Bind off kwise.

HORNS

Make 2
* Cast on 2 sts in white.
* K 1 row.
* Bind off.

MAKING UP

Join the side and top seams of the mask using mattress stitch. Using black yarn, work two French knots for the eyes. Using pale green yarn, work two circles of chain stitch around each eye. Using black yarn, work a triangle of satin stitch for the nose. Work a row of chain stitch at each side of the nose using ocher yarn. Work two French knots for the nostrils using white yarn. Work a row of backstitch for the mouth using red yarn. Work a couple of straight stitches in white yarn for the teeth.

Whipstitch the side seams of the horns and sew them in place.

Cut several lengths of ocher and chunky beige yarn. Sew one small bunch to the top of the head and the other to the chin.

MITTS

Make 2
* Cast on 12 sts in camel.
* K 2 rows.
* Next row: P.
* Work 4 rows in st st, beg with a K row.
* Next row: K1, k2tog, K1, k2tog, ssk, K1, ssk, K1. [8 sts]
* Next row: p2tog, P4, p2tog. [6 sts]
* Break yarn, thread it through rem sts and secure.

MAKING UP

Seam the mitts together using mattress stitch. Using black yarn, work three French knots at the end of each mitt for the claws.

HOW TO KNIT
The Sisters

The world of these selfish sisters seems to be one of constant bad hair days and wardrobe malfunctions. They just couldn't be more different from their beautiful sister, Beauty. The two sisters are knitted identically—the only difference is the colors of the clothes and the color and type of yarn used for the hair. The colors for the second sister are given in parentheses.

MATERIALS

FOR EACH SISTER
¼ oz./8 g (22 yd./20 m) flesh DK yarn

½ oz./14 g (35 yd./32 m) white DK yarn

¼ oz./5 g (13 yd./11.5 m) soft turquoise (orange) DK yarn

½ oz./14.5 g (38 yd./35 m) purple (lime green) DK yarn

⅟₁₆ oz./2.5 g (6 yd./5.5 m) red (bright turquoise) DK yarn

⅛ oz./3.5 g (9 yd./8 m) ocher mohair (rust DK) yarn

Very small amounts of black and red DK yarns

Sewing thread

¾–⅞ oz. (20–25 g) polyester toy filling

FOR THE BLONDE SISTER, YOU WILL ALSO NEED
An elasticated cream bead bracelet

Two pearl buttons

Two brass rings

A store-bought pink ribbon rose

FOR THE RED-HAIRED SISTER, YOU WILL ALSO NEED
An elasticated green bead bracelet

Two crystal-style buttons

Two small pearl beads

A store-bought fabric flower

Use size U.S. 2/3 (3 mm) knitting needles except when instructed to use size U.S. 2 (2.75 mm) knitting needles.

DOLL

HEAD
The head pieces are knitted from the forehead down to the chin.
Make 2 pieces
❊ Cast on 14 sts in flesh.
❊ Work 12 rows in st st, beg with a K row.
❊ Next row: K1, m1, K12, m1, K1. [16 sts]
❊ Work 7 rows in st st, beg with a P row.
❊ Bind off.

BODY

The body is knitted from the lower edge to the neck edge and includes the underpants and bodice of the dress.
Make 2 pieces
❋ Cast on 18 sts in white.
❋ Work 4 rows in st st, beg with a K row.
❋ Break white yarn and join soft turquoise (orange) yarn.
❋ Work 17 rows in st st, beg with a K row.
❋ Next row: K.
❋ Break soft turquoise (orange) yarn and join flesh yarn.
❋ Work 2 rows in st st, beg with a K row.
❋ Next row: Bind off 1 st, K to end. [17 sts]
❋ Next row: Bind off 1 st pwise, P to end. [16 sts]
❋ Bind off.

LEGS

The feet and legs are knitted as one piece, starting at the sole of the foot.
Make 2
❋ Cast on 28 sts in white.
❋ Work 4 rows in st st, beg with a K row.
❋ Next row: K7, bind off 14 sts, K to end. [14 sts]
❋ Work 21 rows in st st, beg with a P row.
❋ Bind off.

ARMS

The arms are knitted from the top of the shoulder to the tip of the hand.
Make 2
❋ Cast on 9 sts in soft turquoise (orange).
❋ Work 2 rows in st st, beg with a K row.
❋ Next row: (K1, m1) to last st, K1. [17 sts]
❋ Work 5 rows in st st, beg with a P row.
❋ Next row: K1, (k2tog) 8 times. [9 sts]
❋ Next row: K.
❋ Break soft turquoise (orange) yarn and join flesh yarn.
❋ Work 13 rows in st st, beg with a K row.
❋ Next row: p2tog, P5, p2tog. [7 sts]
❋ Next row: K1, k2tog, K1, ssk, K1. [5 sts]
❋ Next row: p2tog, P1, p2tog. [3 sts]
❋ Next row: s1, k2tog, psso. [1 st]
❋ Break yarn and pull it through rem st.

MAKING UP

Place the two head pieces right sides together and whipstitch around the edges, leaving the top of the head open for turning and stuffing. Turn the head right side out, stuff, and close the gap using mattress stitch. Sew the body together using mattress stitch, leaving the lower edge open for turning and stuffing. Stuff and close the gap. Sew the head to the body.

Fold one leg in half lengthwise, right sides together, and whipstitch the top and lower edge of the feet. Turn the leg right side out and sew the back seam using mattress stitch. Repeat for the second leg. Stuff the legs and feet.

Fold one arm in half lengthwise, right sides together, and whipstitch around the hand. Turn the arm right side out and sew the long seam using mattress stitch. Repeat for the second arm. Stuff the sleeve part of the arms.

Sew the arms and legs in place.

Cut the yarn for the hair into 27½-in. (70-cm) lengths and gather together in a bunch. Secure the center of the lengths to the top of the head and at each side of the face. Then take the yarn bunches at the sides back to the top of the head and secure again. Braid the ends of the yarn, twist the hair into a bun, and secure.

Work two French knots in black yarn for the eyes. Work a circle of chain stitch around each eye using white yarn. Using a separated ply of black yarn, work four straight stitches above each eye to represent the eyelashes. Using flesh yarn, work two short rows of chain stitch for the nose. To make the nose more prominent, work two more rows of chain stitch on these rows.

Divide a short length of red yarn into two thinner strands. Work two straight stitches to form a V shape for the mouth, then work another two straight stitches over these stitches to make the mouth a little fuller.

Sew the pearl beads or brass rings in position for the earrings using flesh yarn. Sew or glue the flowers in the hair.

Add color to the cheeks using a red colored pencil.

SKIRT OF DRESS

Make 2 pieces
❋ Cast on 30 sts in purple (lime green).
❋ K 2 rows.
❋ Work 4 rows in st st, beg with a P row.
❋ Next row: K.
❋ Next row: K1, (yo, k2tog) to last st, K1.
❋ Next row: K.
❋ Work 14 rows in st st, beg with a K row.
❋ Next row: K2, k2tog, K to last 4 sts, ssk, K2. [28 sts]
❋ Next row: P.
❋ Rep last 2 rows 4 times more. [20 sts]
❋ Bind off pwise.

MAKING UP

Join the side seams of the skirt using mattress stitch. Whipstitch the waist of the skirt in place. Sew the buttons in position.

SHOES

Make 2
❋ Using size U.S. 2 (2.75 mm) needles, cast on 8 sts in red (bright turquoise).
❋ 1st row: inc1, K to last 2 sts, inc1, K1. [10 sts]
❋ Next row: P.
❋ Rep last 2 rows once more. [12 sts]
❋ Work 2 rows in st st, beg with a K row.
❋ Next row: inc1, K to last 2 sts, inc1, K1. [14 sts]
❋ Next row: P5, bind off 4 sts pwise, P to end. Turn work and cont on only these last 5 sts, leaving rem sts on needle or on a safety pin.
❋ Work 8 rows in st st, beg with a K row.
❋ Bind off.
❋ With rs facing, rejoin yarn to rem 5 sts.
❋ Work 8 rows in st st, beg with a K row.
❋ Bind off.

MAKING UP

Fold the shoe pieces in half lengthwise with the right side facing inward. Whipstitch the back and lower seam of the shoes. Turn the right way out. Put the shoes on the doll and secure with a couple of stitches.

INDEX